MR MOJO

A BIOGRAPHY OF JIM MORRISON

DYLAN JONES

BLOOMSBURY

LONDON • NEW DELHI • NEW YORK • SYDNEY

First published in Great Britain in 1991 as *Jim Morrison: Dark Star*.
This revised edition published 2015

Copyright © 1991 and 2015 by Dylan Jones

Bloomsbury Publishing Plc
50 Bedford Square
London
WC1B 3DP

www.bloomsbury.com

Bloomsbury is a trademark of Bloomsbury Publishing Plc
Bloomsbury Publishing, London, New Delhi, New York and Sydney

A CIP catalogue record for this book is available from the British Library

ISBN 978 1 4088 6056 4

10 9 8 7 6 5 4 3 2 1

Typeset by Newgen Knowledge Works (P) Ltd., Chennai, India
Printed and bound in Great Britain by CPI Group (UK) Ltd, Croydon CR0 4YY

For RCB, who certainly wore
leather trousers

Contents

Introduction

At a typical Doors concert, you had two types of crowd. You had the freaks, the heads and the hippies, the longhairs who were tuning in, turning on, and nodding their heads in collective appreciation at the psychedelic and often cacophonous din being made in front of them. They were the ones who stared at album covers to read the track listings to see who had written what.

And then you had the teenage girls, the 'snappers', the ones who sat in the front rows in their high-belted miniskirts and schoolgirl bobby sox, banging their knees together as if they were fanning their insides, trying to get Jim Morrison to stare at their underwear, or – more usually – their lack of. They were the ones who stared at album covers for completely different reasons.

If you look at film performances of the Doors in concert during their heyday, you see a sixties band in all their pomp, effortlessly working their way through their material, determinedly bringing the crowd to whatever climax they had come for. But study the performance a bit more and you see a charismatic frontman, and three musos bent over their instruments who are probably wondering how they got so lucky.

Because the Doors was always three plus one. And the one was always Jim Morrison.

'I think there's a whole region of images and feelings inside us that rarely are given outlet in daily life. And when they do come out, they can take perverse forms. It's the dark side. Everyone, when he sees it, recognises the same thing in himself. It's a recognition of forces that rarely see the light of day.'

Was Jim Morrison joking when he said this?

Morrison was the quintessential sixties pop star – an enigmatic, egotistical playboy with a penchant for philosophical self-absorption and tight black leather trousers. A counter-cultural hero, he physically pushed himself to the limits (he was an alcoholic), exposing his 'dark heart' to a young audience who had only recently recovered from the onslaught of Bob Dylan and the Rolling Stones.

Jim Morrison was something else again. He was Frank Sinatra in leather trousers, an overly theatrical figurehead whose influence can be seen in the personas adopted by everyone from Iggy Pop to Robert Plant, from Patti Smith and Kurt Cobain to Michael Hutchence, Dave Gahan and Brandon Flowers, and every modern version thereof, and whose band delivered the best psychedelic pomp of its day.

He is the narcissistic stuff of rock legend, a self-obsessed drunk whose ridiculous good looks and rich baritone contributed unduly to an archetype that would define both him and every copycat who came in his wake. Not only that, but he was walking around topless while Sting was still in school.

He was the first rock and roll method actor, and would wrap myths around him like a long leather coat, protecting and disguising himself in the process. No literary allusion was too much, no crass putdown too high. He was playing the nascent rock star with such ferocity that it was inevitable he would stumble and fall. And he did petulance better than any entertainer since Marlon Brando.

One of the big problems with Morrison was that he had no ability to manage his success and nor did anyone around him. These days, someone with his talent and his fondness for excessive and seemingly random behaviour would be managed and monitored and pampered and protected during every waking (and sleeping) moment; Morrison was pretty much on his own in a city that was more than happy to live up to its reputation, if not exceed it. Getting lost in LA is easy enough if you're a cosseted twenty-first-century mega-star, but imagine how easy it was for Morrison: all he had to do most days was turn up. It didn't matter if it was turning up at a restaurant, a nightclub, a party, a hotel, an interview, hell, even a recording studio. Wherever he went he was fawned over, feted and fucked up. He was offered all the delights to be found in the most debauched city of the late twentieth century, and with his appetites, he rarely said no.

Why would he? Who would?

'Brian Jones, James Dean, Jimi Hendrix, Jim Morrison, Marc Bolan, Jean-Michel Basquiat, Freddie Mercury, Kurt Cobain are our new immortals,' said Germaine Greer. 'Like Apollo and Dionysus they can never outgrow their dazzling boyhood.'

Hunter S. Thompson called Morrison 'Crazy Jim'. He had 'eyes smarter than James Dean's and a band that could walk with the King, or anybody else. There were some nights when the Doors were the best band in the world. Morrison understood this, and it haunted him all his life. On some nights he was noisy and lewd, and on others he just practised – but every once in a while he would get it into his head to go out and dance with the big boys, and on a night like that he was more than special.'

Morrison used to frequently masturbate onstage, turning away from the audience, then rubbing himself before turning round again, watching the girls who couldn't take their eyes off his engorged cock. He would slide his palm down the front of his leathers, grab his balls and start stroking himself, squeezing his cock and pulling the helmet. He had done it so often that he got hard disturbingly quickly. It was almost as though he had a permanent erection.

A war baby, born in Melbourne, Florida on 8 December 1943, he grew up in the headstrong and affluent fifties, only to rebel against his upbringing a decade later, like so many millions of others. But Morrison was unique, a singer who created a myth around him, a 'dark star' whose shtick was opening up his psyche and inviting the uninitiated to come and peer inside.

With the Doors, whom Joan Didion once called 'the Norman Mailers of the Top 40, missionaries of apocalyptic sex', he created some of the finest pop music of the late sixties, music which still sounds astonishing today, not least because of its lyrical content. Their first two LPs – *The Doors* and *Strange Days* – contain songs that are little more than cleverly constructed vignettes of nihilism set to jaunty tunes – yet they still resonate today. The Doors managed to marry sex appeal, musicianship, and a highly commercial exploitation of undergraduate sensibilities.

A pseudo-intellectual in a snakeskin suit, Morrison always thought he deserved to be something other than a tawdry pop star – he courted film makers and poets, seeing himself as some kind of modern-day Renaissance man, peerless. And that was ultimately his undoing: he ended up tortured by his own image;

bloated by alcohol, despising his audience, hating the tormented Adonis he'd created, the image that had made him successful.

In reality, Morrison was more tormented than anyone knew. He went from being a star trapped inside a boy's body to a man trapped inside his own image. And he was the first rock star to literally self-destruct. Janis Joplin and Jimi Hendrix both died before Morrison, but he was the only one who really needed an escape. Morrison was the first pop star to explore himself (as well as expose himself) in public, and in doing so, went just that little bit too far.

Jim Morrison crammed an awful lot into his twenty-seven years, becoming the most adored American entertainer since Elvis. He had sex, he had drive, he had passion; he had brains, good looks, a voice, a talent for writing evocative, manipulative, nihilistic lyrics and a penchant for Dionysian imagery. He was part poet and part clown, a man who, when he revealed himself, was often to be found simply acting out his own fantasies.

A self-proclaimed 'erotic politician', Morrison was as much a showman as he was a shaman, an actor who pushed his persona as far as it would go. By the time of his 'retirement' in Paris, the Doors were effectively over (although the rest of the group always denied this) and – a sex symbol with a beer belly and a beard – Morrison was toying with the idea of reinventing himself as a poet. The fact that he never did – he was found dead in his bathtub in Paris in July 1971 from an apparent heroin overdose – assured him of immortality and a permanent place in rock and roll's hall of fame. Had he lived, he might undoubtedly have undone all he had achieved during the last five years of his life; as it is, he remains, along with James Dean and Jimi Hendrix, one of youth culture's most revered heroes, a hero dead before his time. A hero who got out just in time.

1

The Ghosts of Père-Lachaise

The easiest way to get to the most famous cemetery in Paris, Père-Lachaise, is to take the Boulevard Périphérique, the continually congested motorway which circles the city. This enormous ring road separates Paris from its suburbs, cutting the capital off from the rest of France. The bane of every Parisian motorist, it nevertheless offers an alternative to the intricate web of narrow streets which weave through the centre of the city. Viewed from the Périphérique, Paris is a fortress, the constant stream of traffic an amorphous mass of frustrated drivers looking for a way in.

It's a typically overcast October weekend, and Paris is cold and grey. Café society has retreated indoors, the trees have all but lost their leaves and the harsh winter is only weeks away. The numbing austerity of motorway concrete leaves you with few expectations.

You leave the Périphérique at Porte de Bagnolet, entering the 20th arrondissement, in the north-west of the city. You weave your way along Rue Belgrand, then Avenue Gambetta, and you find yourself at Père-Lachaise.

This huge municipal necropolis was built soon after the French Revolution by Napoleon, outraged by the thousands of rotting corpses which lay stacked one on top of the other in the small cemeteries of Paris: there was no proper burial ground for the victims of the Reign of Terror. Yet it proved difficult to interest the Parisians in a cemetery which was at that time outside the city and therefore too far to walk for a traditional funeral procession.

In the end a huge publicity campaign was launched, announcing the transfer of various celebrities' remains from their original graves to Père-Lachaise. These included the dramatists Molière and Beaumarchais, the philosopher Abelard and his muse Héloïse, and many others. Even so, Parisians continued to snub the place.

The situation was ultimately saved by Balzac. The popular novelist had the brilliant idea of burying his main characters in Père-Lachaise when they died, and Parisians flocked to the cemetery every Sunday to see for themselves.

Since then it has become France's most star-studded graveyard, a huge monument to creativity, revolution and celebrity: a celebration of both life and death. It includes the graves of Apollinaire, Sarah Bernhardt, Maria Callas, Chopin, Isadora Duncan, Max Ernst, Modigliani, Edith Piaf, Pissarro, Proust, Seurat, Simone Signoret and Oscar Wilde. There are monuments to the Communards of the revolutionary era, and to the millions who died in the Holocaust. Over a million people are buried in Père-Lachaise, and the more famous graves are found among the well-kept tombs of the beloved and the overgrown graves of the forgotten.

Père-Lachaise is a little city, its only living residents the guards and the feral cats who stalk its rambling lanes. And like any city, it has its uptown and its downtown. Uptown are the wide, gravel avenues of marble mausoleums and ornamental family graves covered with huge bouquets of flowers; downtown are the smaller graves, an endless sea of grubby gothic sepulchres looking like row upon row of empty grey stone telephone boxes.

Jim Morrison lives downtown. It's not difficult to find his grave, because there are hundreds of signposts, all handwritten in chalk: 'Jim this way', 'Jim 200 metres', 'This way for the lizard king' – dozens of tiny arrows to help the hordes of visitors on their pilgrimage. The graffiti is overwhelming: 'Anarchy', 'Jim's not dead', 'The Doors are closed', 'Jim, I love you for ever – you will always live in my heart', 'From Italy for Jim

Morrison for ever', 'Jim, love you two times', 'Death give us wings, but he is out of reach', 'Jim, if you leave me, must I come too?' The immediate area surrounding his grave is covered with lyrics from his songs, scrawled in spidery writing or blunt block capitals.

And though it's easy to find, Morrison's grave is quite difficult to see, hidden behind a cluster of narrowly spaced tombs. All that's left is a large block of stone, covered in the inevitable Doors slogans and decorated with a couple of plastic plant pots. For years an alabaster bust graced this box, but it was stolen in May 1988 by two young bandits trying to preserve Morrison's dignity. Disrespectful visitors had chipped away at his face, making him look like a bewigged ghost. For years there were plans to replace the bust with a more fitting tribute.

The grave seems to smell of whisky and nicotine, and the earth surrounding the stone box is littered with bottle tops and cigarette butts.

The tombs on either side of Morrison's grave are constantly cleaned, and most of the graffiti is only a few weeks old. All around, his legacy lives on in badly rendered slogans: a few graves are so damaged that it's difficult to decipher the carved inscriptions, and the trees which line Morrison's avenue have all been carved with knives. Charles Gondouin (died 24 December 1947) must be turning in his grave, as it's his headstone which has suffered the worst abuse. It backs on to Morrison's grave, and has been tagged so many times it looks like the side of a New York subway train.

Decades after his death, Morrison is still pulling in the crowds. Two local boys in leather jackets, T-shirts and blue jeans are sitting on opposite sides of the grave, passing a bottle of beer between them. They smoke cigarettes and stare at the ground. In their own way, they're paying homage to the hedonistic 'Lizard King', letting him know they're on the right course. An upturned whisky bottle has been embedded in the earth and two empty bottles of tequila and Jim Beam Kentucky bourbon have been left on the stone slab – it's these as much as Morrison that the boys seem to be worshipping.

Three Swedish girls wearing backpacks and walking boots stand behind the grave smoking weed as a lone Belgian flips the plastic cork from his bottle of cheap red wine. Gesturing with their hands, they pass the beer, wine and joints between the six of them. Like Morrison himself, his fans are indiscriminate drinkers. Every few minutes someone else arrives, joining the crowd around the tiny monument. They examine the graffiti, take photographs of themselves on the grave (usually wearing sunglasses), and bask in the strange air of reverence. More people arrive, another joint is passed around, and the day rolls on.

Every twenty minutes or so the security guards pass by. They shoo people off the graves and retrieve the discarded liquor bottles and food wrappers, like any disgruntled park keeper. Occasionally the gendarmes pay a visit. They frisk undesirables, confiscate any alcohol and move people on. On the twelfth anniversary of Morrison's death in 1983 the police had to use tear gas to break up a group of mourners. A few years ago Morrison's grave was the focal point for Parisian juvenile delinquency, a popular place for wild parties and debauchery. People would gather here during the day and at night after the cemetery closed, to play guitars, have sex, buy drugs or just hang out. But the police stopped all that, and regularly patrol the graveyard in the hope of rounding up any suspicious characters who haven't got the message.

Père-Lachaise has become just another stop on the backpackers' tour of Europe, like the Pompidou Centre, the Eiffel Tower or the Grande Arche at La Défense. There are still those who make the pilgrimage because they are Doors fanatics, or because Morrison is their idol, but usually the visitors are there out of idle curiosity. If you're 'doing Paris' then you have to visit Père-Lachaise. The grave is still a shrine, but it has become a meeting place for tourists, like London's Carnaby Street or Covent Garden.

Twenty-year-old Jacqui is from Sydney. She's here because to her Jim Morrison represents the ideology and the freedom of the sixties. 'And', she says, 'he was a pretty cool guy. Very sexy. I'm surprised by the grave, though – it's very bare, very poor. I thought it would be much more elaborate. The bottles on the grave are very symbolic. I've just had a drink sitting on the grave – that felt very cool! I'll definitely come again if I come back to Paris – you know, pay my respects, have another drink, and another smoke! They say he's still alive, making music with Elvis in Africa, but I don't know ...'

Lee Demelo, twenty-two, is from Ontario, touring Europe for the first time, stopping off in Paris for two weeks. 'Basically we've seen all the sights and we wanted to take a day off to come here, because it's the thing to do. It's not what I expected, you know? You walk in here and there's all these humungous tombstones, and you walk up to Jim Morrison's grave and there's nothing, really. I suppose it's not important, right? It's just the mental concept that this is where he's buried, or supposed to be buried, right? All the people at the youth hostel have been here. It's great – I'm the only person out of all my friends from Canada who's been to Paris, and I'll be able to go back and brag about how I went to Jim Morrison's grave. That's cool. We've taken some pictures to prove we've been here.

'He means so much to people, you know? The Doors' albums still sell, and they still mean a lot to people. They're not like one of those groups that come and go ... they'll always be there. I'm not really a Top-40 kinda guy, and the Doors mean a lot to me.'

Blue is an ageing French teacher who lived in Paris at the same time as Morrison. She has brought a single red rose to adorn his grave. 'I've been about a dozen times since he died – whenever I'm in Paris I make a point of coming here. I come because to a certain extent he represented our generation. I was never a fan of his music but I liked his poems – and I could see he was trying to do something new with his poetry. But no one ever understood him, and he started to manipulate people when he didn't become appreci-ated. I know a girl who knew him closely, and she said he was more concerned about his poetry than he was about anything else he did. When he got them published he was happier than when he got his first record release.

'It's a pity he became so manipulative, because I really think he had something, but he turned into quite a monster, I think. A shame.'

By now there are twenty people mingling around the grave, swapping stories, drinks and telephone numbers. There's Adam from Iowa, Jim and Sheila from Birmingham, England, Bruce and Mikey from San Francisco, and a gaggle of college students from Los Angeles. Three middle-aged Parisian women sit on a nearby grave, sharing a bottle of cheap cognac and talking about nothing in particular. No one there knew Morrison, but this is the place to be. Two boys and a girl sit opposite, collectively rolling a joint. They finish a packet of Camel filters before smoking it. Natalie, Fred and Oliver all live nearby, and come to the cemetery every day. They always meet at Morrison's grave, because, they say, 'We like his history, he was a rebel.' They're thinking of not coming any more, because the place is always swamped by tourists. 'And the police come every five minutes,' says Natalie, 'it's getting to be a drag. I'm not sure if it's cool to hang out here anymore.'

A frail-looking couple dressed entirely in black amble up to the throng. The boy holds a bunch of flowers. They stare for a minute and then start to walk away. 'The flowers are for Oscar Wilde,' says Jeremy, a nineteen-year-old from Manhattan. The girl, also from New York, is called Kris. 'Jim Morrison gets all the attention,' she says, 'so we thought we'd visit Wilde. Anyway, it looks like we're gatecrashing a party here.'

Photographers and backpackers come and go, cautiously approaching the grave in case they're intruding; some scan the cemetery guide, perhaps wondering why Morrison's name is misspelt Morisson; the security guards drive past again and the day draws to a close. It seems like Morrison's grave is the longest running open-air nightclub in Europe.

As the wind gets up, Blue slowly turns to say goodbye. 'I don't think I'll be coming again,' she says. 'This place is like a garbage tip now.'

There are as many rumours about Jim Morrison's death as there are about his life. Not only are the circumstances in which he died incredibly suspect, but so are the many things which are supposed to have befallen him since. You can take your pick: he is still alive; his body was stolen by friends soon after his death and shipped back to California; he was cremated and his ashes eventually smoked by Morrison's Parisian heroin dealer; his ashes were scattered over the Seine. One journalist was even told by a guard at Père-Lachaise that Morrison's family came and collected the body at the beginning of the eighties. Graffiti near the grave states, 'We came to see you, Jim, even though we know you're not there' – but this is wishful thinking. By keeping their options open Morrison obsessives can perpetuate the myth, which becomes dramatically less mysterious if you believe he is buried at Père-Lachaise. But there seems little doubt that he is.

Monsieur Forestier, the custodian of the cemetery, was shocked when asked whether Morrison was buried there. 'Of course he's there, he's always been there. Only the bust has been removed.' He even refutes the story about the family retrieving the body: 'Even they can't take away the body, they're officially not allowed to. You can't just pick up bodies and move them somewhere else. He's here.'

Should we believe this? Certainly the custodians of Père-Lachaise didn't have the same qualms when they moved Molière, Beaumarchais and Abelard to attract attention to their cemetery; and bodies are moved from cemeteries all the time (often to make way for real estate). It's also possible that Admiral Steve Morrison's contacts allowed him to secretly move his son's body back to the USA.

But if Morrison's body isn't there, why do they claim it is? One of the most densely populated cemeteries in the world, Père-Lachaise is not starved of tourists, and the graves of Oscar Wilde and Edith Piaf alone would keep it full of visitors. It's not as if the authorities need Jim Morrison. The surrounding graves have to be regularly cleaned, and the guards could find better things to do with their time than patrol Morrison's tomb on the lookout for deviants. Monsieur Forestier simply doesn't need the trouble, so why should he lie?

Two hours later the grave is littered with flowers: small bunches of tulips and individually packed red roses. Pinet Fleurs, the florist next door to the entrance to the cemetery in Boulevard de Ménilmontant, say they sell flowers to Morrison-mourners every day of the year.

As you leave the cemetery the graffiti continues: 'The Doors are for ever, not some fast trend', 'I ask this of you, Jim, is this the end?', 'Fuck it all', 'Jim, dead but not gone', 'Some oysters for you, Jim', 'Jim, we party for you for ever', 'Jim, Becky from Crystal Lake, Illinois,

Loves You'. There is graffiti from all over the world – cryptic little messages in Italian, French, German, Spanish, personal pleas from Australia, America, Canada and Britain. The final message, scrawled on a plastic rubbish bin opposite the Métro, is written in thick black felt-tip: 'Jim stinks', it says.

2

The New Californians

Today in Los Angeles, the sixties are still very much alive and kicking – if you know where to look, that is. Laurel Canyon is often written about as the place that gave the world Crosby, Stills & Nash, the place that inspired Joni Mitchell's 'Ladies of the Canyon', Danny Sugerman's *Wonderland Avenue*. It is a neighbourhood of benign bad behaviour and clandestine misdemeanours. Everyone from Clara Bow and Christina Applegate to Frank Zappa and Marilyn Manson has lived there, and it retains a genuine local feel – almost impossible in LA. This being Los Angeles, the area has also had its fair share of dark moments, not least the Wonderland murders, which happened in 1981, when four people were bludgeoned to death with striated steel pipes in a drug-related plot that involved the porn star John Holmes.

Despite being the subject of standard-issue gentrification, the Canyon has kept the funky, rainbow-coloured charm of the Love Generation, something that is most apparent when visiting the Canyon Country Store, still the neighbourhood's social hub. Wedged along the twisting Laurel Canyon Boulevard in the Santa Monica Mountains between West Hollywood and the San Fernando Valley, this is the place mentioned in Jim Morrison's 'Love Street' ('I see you live on Love Street, There's this store where the creatures meet'). In fact the song was completely based around the store; Morrison would spend days hanging out there, loafing around outside, sitting on an orange crate, staring at girls and drinking from a bottle of Scotch. For years the graffiti MR MOJO RISIN' graced the front of the store. The wooden-floored grocery shop /café is still the place to go for canyon dwellers with the munchies, or for those in the industry who aren't working, and who need somewhere in the morning to stop for an espresso having spent all night partying in the Valley. Here they'll find Dandy Don's ice cream, Dave's Kombucha (fermented tea), bespoke sandwiches, hearts of palm salads, and the almost-but-not-quite-legendary decaf almond-milk latte. Run out of Californian chardonnay, Heinz baked beans, Daddy's Sauce or patchouli incense? Look no further.

The Country Store is also the site of the annual Photo Day each October, where the residents of the

Canyon all come together to have a group picture taken. The tradition dates back to the late eighties, a celebration of the sort of community spirit you don't find anywhere else in LA.

Over the hill, the temporal nature of Hollywood is at its most obvious. Here, in the village of bougain-villea and watery melodies, time stands still. And if you want to wear your bellbottoms and feathers, don't think twice, it's all right. This is where so many people ended up when they moved to LA in the mid-sixties. Sure, there were many more who ended up living in squalor in East Hollywood, and even more whose living arrangements involved the wrong end of Sunset Boulevard (where the house numbers are broken into fractions), but the canyons between LA and the Ventura are where so many wanderers made their home. New wanderers!

That was the thing about the sixties: everybody was new. No one had been around for a while – no one had been loitering around for five, ten years – no one had been hovering on the edge of the scene, desperate for a flash of fairy dust, as there hadn't actually *been* a scene. There had been such a flight to California, such a migra-tion, that the state was suddenly full of young people searching for a future. These were not Okies seeking jobs, land or dignity; these were teenagers looking for reinvention. If the dust bowl farmers brought country music to California, the teenage prodigies who descended on San Francisco and Los Angeles helped build a bucolic haven that soon became the centre of the counter-cultural universe. If London had invented the modern 'scene' at the start of the sixties, the second half of the decade belonged to California.

Everyone here was here for the first time. Here, having escaped the dull ceiling of a sky that stretched all the way from Chicago to New York, the newly arrived smartly dressed denizens of Haight-Ashbury and Laurel Canyon were all afflicted with blind optimism. Now that they were all in California, what was the worst that could happen? And here, as if in the middle of some bizarre Darwinian experiment, this loose amalgamation of outsiders – hellions, even – gradually became less and less like the people they'd left behind, and more and more like . . . well, Californians . . . New Californians!

Like E. B. White's new New Yorkers, these recently arrived Los Angelenos were seeking sanctuary or fulfilment or some greater or lesser grail. White said that no one should come to New York to live unless they are willing to be lucky; luck was even more important in LA. Whether they wore tie-dye T-shirts or satin suits festooned with flowers, California's beautiful people were as one – eager participants in bespoke bacchanalia. Like a line from the Leiber and Stoller song 'Fools Fall in Love', they built their castle on wishes with only rainbows for beams.

During the spring of 1965, people all over America began migrating to Los Angeles, eager to bathe in the soporific glow of the lifestyle revolution and bask in the emerging bohemian culture. The city quickly acquired its own band of freaks, dressed in jerkins, knee-breeches, knitted shawls, Indian beads, old lace dresses and flowered shirts. Musicians, artists, actors, film makers, sculptors, designers, bikers, hedonists, hippies: the synthesis of the West Coast social revolution.

But unlike San Francisco, where altruism was the order of the day, Los Angeles produced a kind of venal synaesthesia, a sensory overload. As Lawrence Dietz described the scene, writing in *Cheetah* magazine: 'You go out to Los Angeles from the East, and of course you have heard all of these funny stories about the funny natives, and all of the funny things they're into, and it takes some time for you to realise that everyone out there is playing this whole new game. Everyone is searching for what you might call self-realisation of one sort or another. In LA everyone is into himself, in one way or another.'

Some were there by accident, others by design, but all by default. The whole of LA was in a frenzy; a frenzy compounded by heat, fame, drugs and life on the beach. LSD was becoming the sacrament of the city, and it was said that being in LA was like being high all the time. One of the new wave of beatniks who flocked to Los Angeles was a twenty-one-year-old college student called Jim Morrison. He arrived in the spring of 1964 fresh from Florida State University, keen to embroil himself in modern America's fairy-tale city of light. He journeyed to California – against his parents' wishes – to reinvent himself. He wasn't looking to drop out – he would have gone to San Francisco for that. The budding boho was looking to drop in, to be accepted by the new bohemians. Soon he would begin to feed off the city, letting it wrap itself around him, letting its warm neon flow through his veins. But for the time being he threw himself into his work, casting himself as a student of film. Jim Morrison's own movie was unfolding.

According to legend, the Jim Morrison movie really began in 1947, when he was four years old. While driving through the New Mexico desert, the Morrison family came across a horrendous road accident, an event which would cause severe repercussions in Jim's life, and one to which he would constantly refer in his poems. Morrison was convinced that at the age of four the soul of a dead Pueblo Indian entered his body, altering the course of his life: a more than suitable beginning for a movie.

'The first time I discovered death,' said Morrison, 'me and my mother and father, and my grandmother and grandfather, were driving through the desert at dawn. A truckload of Indians had either hit another car or something – there were Indians scattered all over the highway, bleeding to death. So we pulled the car up . . . I don't remember if I'd ever been to a movie, and suddenly, there were all these redskins, and they're lying all over the road, bleeding to death. I was just a kid, so I had to stay in the car while my father and grandfather went back to check it out . . . I didn't see nothing – all I saw was funny red paint and people lying around, but I knew something was happening, because I could dig the vibrations of the people around me, 'cause they're my parents and all, and all of a sudden I realised that they didn't know what was happening any more than I did. That was the first time I tasted fear . . . and I do think, at that moment, the soul or the ghosts of those dead Indians, maybe one or two of 'em, were just running around, freaking out, and just landed in my soul, and I was like a sponge, ready to just sit there and absorb it . . . It's not a ghost story, it's something that really means something to me.'

Jim Morrison was the son of a high-ranking naval officer, born into a family with a long history of career militarists. James Douglas was Steve and Clara Morrison's first child, a bright, healthy baby with fat cheeks and cold, sparkling eyes. Soon after Jim was born, Steve Morrison was posted to the Pacific, where he stayed for three years, entrenched in a war of attrition with the Japanese. His father away at war, the boy spent the first three years of his life with his mother at his paternal grandparents' house, in Clearwater, on the

Gulf coast of Florida. When he eventually returned from the war, in the humid summer of 1946, Steve Morrison's family began a gypsy-like existence, first moving to Washington DC for six months, and then to Albuquerque, New Mexico, for a year. During the next fifteen years, Morrison senior was sent all over America, and was often away from home on manoeuvres, leaving the boy to be brought up by Clara. If little Jim needed a father figure, he certainly didn't get one.

The family kept on moving: early in 1948, Steve Morrison took his family to Los Altos in northern California, where they were stationed for nearly four years. Then it was back to Washington DC for a year (while Steve was stationed in Korea), then Claremont, California, for another two. Along the way little Jim acquired a sister, Ann, and a brother, Andrew. And still they kept on moving: when Morrison senior returned from Korea, they went back to Albuquerque for two years before moving on to San Francisco. In December 1958, they returned to Washington, where they stayed for three years, and where Jim attended George Washington High School.

Although his family were conventional, middle-class Republicans, with solid, traditional, patriarchal values, little Jim's stability was constantly threatened by this continual uprooting. Life in the services offered welcome financial security in the fifties, but it hardly fostered emotional stability. Morrison was always rootless, and soon developed a shield and a way of responding to people with whom he knew his relationship would be brief. Without a peer group to call his own, he remodelled himself wherever he went – a chameleon with a satchel.

Morrison grew up quickly. In adolescence he discovered a gregarious side to his nature, and developed an extreme way of dealing with the world. He wanted to be liked, and the easiest way was to show off by acting the fool or performing outrageous stunts. Morrison was already behaving in a resolutely odd manner, and each new set of classmates quickly learned to avoid the nascent rebel. He was also discovering a Machiavellian streak in himself, finding it easy to manipulate his school friends, and a sick sense of humour was beginning to manifest itself. Morrison could be deliberately mysterious, and was already acquiring an armoury of masks.

It was at George Washington High that the softly spoken and articulate sophomore began writing poetry. He discovered he was adept with words, and started to keep a diary and write short stories. He immersed himself in his books. He had a formidable capacity for learning, and devoured William Blake, Jack Kerouac, Allen Ginsberg, Colin Wilson, Aldous Huxley, Sartre and Rimbaud, while at the same time developing a taste for beer. He was soon fascinated by the romantic notion of poetry, as Jerry Hopkins and

Danny Sugerman point out in their biography, *No One Here Gets Out Alive*. 'To be a poet entailed more than writing poems. It demanded a commitment to live, and die, with great style and even greater sadness; to wake each morning with the fever raging and know it would never be extinguished except by death, yet to be convinced that this suffering carried a unique reward.'

This was something to which Morrison could aspire. The tortured artist? Sure, he could do that, no problem. But although he was alarmingly intelligent and a gifted, if lazy, student, Morrison was completely indifferent to any possibilities of a long-term career. Being remarkably bright, the Navy brat didn't have to study much to achieve high marks and consistently got good grades, even though he spent most of his time reading poetry, writing his diary or getting drunk. His parents, sensing his apathy, enrolled him in St Petersburg Junior College in Florida, informing him that he had to live with his grandparents in Clearwater. Morrison reluctantly co-operated, and in September 1961, while the rest of the family travelled to San Diego, he moved to the Sunshine State. After an unremarkable year he transferred to Florida State University in Tallahassee, before dropping out and forcing his parents to allow him to switch to UCLA to study film in early 1964.

Morrison had been fascinated by cinema since his early teens, though the transfer to UCLA was as much about moving to Los Angeles as it was about studying film. And although he hurled himself into the course, it was his first experiments with drugs that really fuelled Morrison's thoughts. Twelve frustrating and uneventful months later he was gone. After receiving negative grades for his end-of-term film, he quit college and disappeared to the beach. His project, a free-form short with no discernible script, was, to quote Morrison, 'a film questioning the film process itself . . . a film about film'. In reality it was a series of abstract and surreal images stuck together like a proto-pop video. Nazi soldiers were juxtaposed with the title sequence from the TV show *The Outer Limits*, as the cameraman's girlfriend jumped about in bra, panties and high heels. This medley of meaningless images failed to impress Morrison's tutors, who gave him a 'complimentary D'. Throughout his short career, his lyrics and poems would allude to the cinema, and when he finally got around to making films himself, they were heavily self-referential.

Having lost his student deferment, Morrison was now a prime candidate for military service, so to escape the draft he moved to Venice, an early cradle of hippiedom on the ocean-front south of Santa Monica. From June 1964 to August 1965 he shared an apartment with another student from his film course, all the time increasing his use of alcohol and drugs. LSD was still legal at the time, and Morrison made the most of it, by his own admission swallowing acid 'like candy'.

Having already stretched his mind through books, he now wanted to expand it even further, by pummelling it with drugs. It was during this period that he wrote most of the songs which would appear on the first two Doors LPs, songs inspired by Huxley, Blake, Céline and the other writers he had studied in school.

'I was hearing in my head a whole concert situation, with a band and an audience. Those first five or six songs I wrote, I was just really taking notes at this fantastic rock concert that was going on inside my head . . . and once I'd written these songs, I just had to sing them. The music came first, and then I'd make up some words to hang on the melody, and because that was the only way I could remember it, and most of the time I'd end up with just the words and forget the tune. I'd been going to school or college constantly for fifteen years, it was a beautiful, hot summer and I just started hearing songs.'

Morrison had recently met Chicago-born Ray Manzarek, a fellow film student and prodigious classical pianist who played in a blues band called Rick and the Ravens with his brothers in a bar in Santa Monica at weekends. Like many Americans of his age, ever since he'd witnessed the British invasion, Manzarek had wanted to be a rock star: 'We saw the Beatles and the Rolling Stones and thought – wait a minute, these guys are art students like us. Are you kiddin'? These people are front page news! People are going crazy over them! Girls are throwing themselves at them. They're making records; they're making money. We want this too!'

Manzarek's band were billed to support Sonny and Cher at a graduation hop, and Manzarek asked Morrison to step in and replace their guitarist, so that they could make up the six musicians required in the contract. Unable to play an instrument, Jim made his debut performance standing at the back of the stage with his back to the audience, an unplugged guitar over his shoulder. Looking as mean and moody as he could, Morrison was Stuart Sutcliffe incarnate. He had at last found an actor to play the lead role in his movie.

While Morrison loved rock and roll – 'It opened up a whole new world that I wasn't aware of – a free, exciting, strange, tense landscape' – and was particularly interested in the blues, he had never entertained the idea of becoming a singer. It took the hot summer of 1965 and a lot of acid to convince him that music could become a vehicle for his poetry. Morrison was also becoming more aware of himself physically, realising he was turning into a seriously attractive twenty-one-year-old. He'd initially been hurt by the film school's rejection, but as his self-confidence grew, the idea of becoming a rock singer became increasingly plausible. He could be a film maker some other time.

Then came another fateful meeting with Ray Manzarek. '[It was] a beautiful California summer day, the middle of August, and who should come walking down the beach but Jim Morrison. I said, "Hey man, I thought you were going to New York," and he said, "Well, I was, but I decided to stay here. I've been at a friend's house, up on his rooftop, writing songs."'

Morrison then started singing 'Moonlight Drive', and Manzarek was hooked. 'When I heard those first four lines, I said, "Wow, that's it – those are the best lyrics I've ever heard for a rock'n'roll song!" As he was singing, I could hear the chord changes and the beat: my fingers immediately started moving.'

Manzarek asked if he had any others, and Morrison sung a few more. Manzarek seized the opportunity, and told Morrison they should form a group.

When they met that day, Manzarek said Morrison looked like Michelangelo's David, having lost his puppy fat and found his cheekbones. As he'd been living off little but acid for the past few months, he was incredibly gaunt, his weight having dropped from 160 pounds to under 135. The transformation was nearly complete.

The pair then recruited a drummer called John Densmore whom Manzarek had met in his meditation class. At first the sober and untroubled Californian had reservations about the partnership: 'Their songs were really far out to me . . . I didn't understand very much; but then I figured, I'm the drummer, not the lyricist.' Nevertheless, he joined.

Morrison set about turning the group into a vehicle for his ideas. In the spirit of the times, he became obsessed with subversion: 'America was conceived in violence. Americans are attracted to violence, out of cans. They're TV-hypnotised – TV is the invisible protective shield against bare reality. Twentieth-century culture's disease is the inability to feel any reality. People cluster to TV, soap operas, movies, theater, pop idols, and they have wild emotion over symbols. But in the reality of their own lives, they're emotionally dead.'

Morrison was also obsessed with what he called the 'Apollonian–Dionysian split'. The idea came from Nietzsche, who devoted much time to analysing the phenomenon in Greek culture. The German philosopher's book *The Birth of Tragedy*, written in 1872, was once cited by Morrison as the volume to read if you wanted to understand his thoughts. It is, to quote Morrison biographer Mike Jahn, 'a philosophical road map to the Doors'. The terms are derived from the names of the Greek gods Apollo and Dionysus. As well as being the messenger of the gods, Apollo was the presiding deity of music, medicine, light and youth, and was identified with the sun. The handsome, youthful, long-haired Dionysus was the god of wine and permissiveness, universally adored by women. It's no wonder Morrison chose to identify with him.

Nietzsche used these terms to make a distinction between reason and instinct, between order and chaos. Apollonian culture produced order and control, whereas Dionysian culture encouraged emotional abandon. 'Under the charm of the Dionysian,' wrote Nietzsche, 'not only is the union between man and man reaffirmed, but nature which has become alienated, hostile or subjugated, celebrates once more her reconciliation with her lost son, man.' When he pointed out that music and theatre were the natural expressions of the Dionysian, Morrison took the bait, hook, line and sinker.

Morrison often referred to the Doors as a theatre of myths, always stressing the Greek connection. 'Sometimes I like to look at the history of rock and roll like the origin of Greek drama,' he once said, 'which started out of a threshing floor at the crucial seasons and was originally a band of worshippers, dancing and singing. Then, one day, a possessed person jumped out of the crowd and started imitating a god.'

In September 1965 Morrison met an eighteen-year-old redhead called Pamela Courson, a typically pretty California girl, whose father was also an officer in the Naval Reserve. Just before meeting Morrison she had dropped out of her art classes at Los Angeles City College, and was 'looking for something meaningful to do'. In Jim Morrison she found it. The couple fell in love, soon becoming inseparable. Jim would often refer to Pamela as his 'cosmic mate', and their relationship continued right up until his death. For Morrison it was a perversely normal relationship – he read her his poems and lectured her on what books to read, while she taught him how to dress. And together they plunged into Mondo Hollywood.

By the end of 1965, Los Angeles was awash with freaks. Every proto-hipster came equipped with his own emotional baggage and newly adopted convictions. Every new arrival had an angle; Morrison's was poetry. Pamela Zarubica (aka Suzy Creamcheese), the infamous Frank Zappa acolyte, remembers Morrison's arrival, courting the famous and the influential, the notorious and the hip, desperate to be liked: 'That Jim Morrison sure was a drag, always play-acting and making everybody listen to his poems.' Captain Beefheart (Don van Vliet), a genuine Californian bohemian, was amused by Morrison's lust for approval. He remembers him turning up in LA, looking like a weekend hippie, with his very own 'bongo speech', gauche and eager to make friends, trying to penetrate the underbelly of hip LA.

By fleeing to LA, Morrison left behind his white-bread upbringing. Dismissive of the cradle-to-grave security of his father's world, he revamped himself for public consumption. To quote journalist Mick Farren, LA 'provided him with a backdrop to act out his fantasies'. The Los Angeles that Morrison found was a movie set full of failed actors, freaks, beatniks, weirdos and drug fiends. If San Francisco had the ultimate utopian Zeitgeist, Los Angeles was a more hungry city, a town where fame and fortune were still desirable, tangible things. LA was the ultimate synthetic city, an unholy sprawling town with no real sense of community. In LA, people didn't understand good or evil – only success or failure. Many had come looking for fame and fortune, though few had been chosen. The unlucky ones were destined to prowl the bars along Sunset Strip, dreaming of what might have been.

Morrison the actor was at home in LA. In San Francisco his dreams would have appeared callous and shallow, but in a city full of aspiring luminaries his ambitions weren't noticed. He had found his city. LA was the twentieth-century manifestation of the Apollonian–Dionysian split, where reality and unreality went side by side, bumper to bumper: the rich and the poor, the famous and the invisible.

Morrison naturally gravitated towards the hipper, seamier side of the city, hanging out with winos and hookers, as well as with the young hippies who littered the beaches and the bars. He could remake himself here, he thought, and no one would notice, because no one particularly cared; in LA, everyone looked out for himself.

Before Manzarek was lucky enough to hook up with Morrison, Rick and the Ravens had signed a contract with Aura Records. Their first single died, so rather than release another potential disaster, Aura offered them free studio time. The Ravens, who were practically now the Doors, gratefully accepted. One September evening in 1965 the group spent three hours in World Pacific Studios on 3rd Street recording six prototype Doors songs: 'Hello I Love You', 'Moonlight Drive', 'My Eyes Have Seen You', 'End of the Night', 'Summer's Almost Gone' and 'Go Insane' (which was later incorporated into 'The Celebration of the Lizard'). They hawked the demos around to various record companies, until Columbia eventually offered them a small deal.

Morrison called the band the Doors in homage to William Blake and Aldous Huxley; Blake had written, 'If the doors of perception were cleansed, everything would appear to man as it truly is, infinite,' which inspired the title of Huxley's book about his mystical experiences with mescaline, *The Doors of Perception* (1954). For a cocky college kid who wanted to be a rock star, the name had all the right cultural connotations.

Morrison then set about moulding his band into the kind of vehicle he felt comfortable with. The cover versions slowly began to disappear, and all of a sudden the band stopped smiling onstage. This was an important turning point: how could you peddle esoteric, philosophical rock if you looked happy about it?

Columbia had taken the bait, but Ray's brothers decided to leave, unsure about the group's new direction. Short of a guitarist, they recruited the mild-mannered Robby Krieger, a friend of John Densmore (they had played together in a band called the Psychedelic Rangers) and a member of John and Ray's meditation class. A native of Los Angeles, Krieger was studying psychology at UCLA. He was only nineteen, the youngest in the group. Krieger's was a highly original guitar sound, an idiosyncratic, folk-based noise, and he often used a bottleneck (preserved for posterity on 'Moonlight Drive', the first song all four Doors played together).

The band honed their sound during their many gigs in the LA area, though at this time Manzarek did most of the singing, Morrison standing with his back to the audience, too shy to perform to anyone other than his friends. They played bar mitzvahs, birthdays, weddings – any gig they could get. They really wanted a residency at a club, but were turned down by all of them because they didn't have a bass player. Just as they were about to recruit one, Manzarek stumbled upon a Fender Rhodes piano bass being played by the house band in one of the many clubs they auditioned for.

The piano bass sounded like a bass guitar but played like a keyboard, and as Manzarek had been trained in the boogie-woogie, stride-piano technique (in which the hands work almost independently of each other), he decided to use it in the band. And so the Doors' sound was born: Morrison's throaty baritone vocals; Krieger's intricate, clean guitar; Densmore's sharp, unobtrusive drums; and Manzarek's oceanic keyboards.

They were now playing crisp, jazzy, white-boy blues – sensual, cinematic vignettes dramatised by Morrison's primordial lyrics.

The more concerts the Doors played, the more confident Morrison became onstage. And as he started being pursued by the gangs of girls who were now appearing in the audience, so he grew into his image. Morrison soon discovered he could be sexy as well as brainy.

After rehearsing for three months, in January 1966 the Doors finally got their residency, and were lucky enough to become the house band at the London Fog, a small, sleazy club near the Whisky a Go Go on Sunset Strip. The Fog was usually frequented by drunks, hookers, sailors and the occasional hipster – the kind of habitual fly-by-nights who weren't interested in the textural subtleties of a band like the Doors. As far as they were concerned, the four long-haired college students up on the stage were a bar band, good and simple. But the Doors thrived. Just like the Beatles in Hamburg, they would play four or five sets a night, starting at nine and continuing until two or three in the morning with fifteen-minute breaks in between.

It was in this atmosphere that the band developed their sound, perfecting new material like 'Light My Fire', 'Hello I Love You', 'Break On Through' and 'Waiting for the Sun', songs which would serve them well on their first three albums. They knew these songs so well that when they came to record them they did it almost live. And because they played so often they were able to experiment continually, allowing themselves the luxury of long instrumental breaks. They played the London Fog for four months, making $5 each per night and $10 at weekends.

The Doors' relationship with Columbia was brief, and they were soon dropped. They were also dropped by the Fog, though they were signed up almost immediately by the prestigious Whisky a Go Go, becoming the house band and opening for Buffalo Springfield, Captain Beefheart, Them, Love, the Turtles and the Byrds. The band played there for three months, earning $125 each a week. They soon gained a reputation for playing too loud and attempting to blow the headlining act offstage. They also started to attract a small crowd who would turn up night after night to see them. Morrison was now the star attraction, having learned to love the spotlight. He would often turn up drunk, stoned or both, though unsurprisingly this only endeared him to the band's growing audience.

It was at the Whisky that they were first seen by Jac Holzman, the founder and president of Elektra Records, an independent New York company mostly known for its folk-rock catalogue. Elektra had recently signed Arthur Lee's psychedelic quintet Love, and was looking to sign up other rock acts. After a few return visits, Holzman offered to sign the Doors. Although desperate for a deal, the band nevertheless played it cool. But secretly they were more than pleased with the proposition – Elektra had the integrity that a lot of the major labels lacked, and the deal gave them almost complete control over their output. They soon signed. The timing was right, as they had recently been fired from the Whisky, too. One night Morrison, blitzed on LSD, decided to improvise during one of their longer songs, 'The End'. Digging through his library books, he came up with a trite spoken passage steeped in Freudian theory: 'Father,' Morrison shouted from the stage. 'Yes son . . . I want to kill you . . . Mother . . . I want to . . . FUCK YOU!' He had been orchestrating silences, screams and manic outbursts during most of the band's recent performances, but this was a primal scream to end them all. The audience were shocked; the management, appalled, fired the band.

Ray Manzarek described how the song developed. '"The End" was originally a very short piece, but because of all the time we had to fill onstage, we started extending songs, taking them into areas that we didn't know they would go into . . . and playing stoned every night. It was the great summer of acid, and we really got into a lot of improvisation, and I think the fact that no one was at the club really helped us to develop what the Doors became.'

A year before, the band had sounded like any other beat combo, but now, with Morrison writing nearly all of their songs, the Doors were firmly entrenched in the emerging drug culture. Morrison's songs were often incongruous and demanding, but they were written like advertising copy: concise and compact.

Encouraged by the group's success, he began incorporating more and more philosophical and mythological references into the songs, drawing on his considerable literary knowledge. Those days in the library hadn't been wasted, as he now used his wide reading to build himself a career, page by page.

Morrison's creativity was helped by his staggering drug intake: his experiments with LSD, peyote, grass and alcohol. He still had nowhere to live, preferring to wander the streets of West Los Angeles, looking for kicks and sleeping rough. By comparison the rest of the group were clean-living, and their drug-taking never seemed to interfere with their day job. But drugs now fuelled Morrison's work, and he began more and more to rely on them to keep himself sane. Success was only just around the corner, and he had to be prepared.

Morrison saw himself as a Dionysian, and may well have believed himself to be testing the reality of Rimbaud's assertion that a poet becomes a visionary through 'a long, boundless and systematic disordering of the senses' – a creed, to quote writer Mick Brown, 'which has percolated into rock and roll as the mythology of romantic self-destruction'.

His 'Big Thing', to which he constantly referred in both song and interview, was the confrontation of reality. A typical explanation would go something like this: 'People are afraid of themselves – of their own reality – their feelings most of all. People talk about how great love is, but that's bullshit. Love hurts. Feelings are disturbing. People are taught that pain is evil and dangerous. How can they deal with love if they're afraid to feel? Pain is meant to wake us up. People try to hide their pain. But they're wrong. Pain is something to carry, like a radio. You feel your strength in the experience of pain. It's all in how you carry it. That's what matters. Pain is a feeling – your feelings are a part of you. Your own reality. If you feel ashamed of them, and hide them, you're letting society destroy your reality. You should stand up for your right to feel your pain.'

'Sometimes the pain is too much to examine, or even tolerate,' he said, explaining the meaning of the line, 'My only friend, the End'. 'That doesn't make it evil, though – or necessarily dangerous. But people fear death even more than pain. It's strange that they fear death. Life hurts a lot more than death. At the point of death, the pain is over. Yeah – I guess it is a friend . . .'

When he began to be probed by journalists, Morrison found he had an answer for everything: 'If you reject your body, it becomes your prison cell. It's a paradox – to transcend the limitations of the body, you have to immerse yourself in it – you have to be totally open to your senses . . . It isn't easy to accept your body – we're taught that the body is something to control, dominate – natural processes like pissing and shitting are considered dirty . . . Puritanical attitudes die slowly. How can sex be a liberation if you don't really want to touch your body – if you're trying to escape from it?'

Sex and death motifs, enigmatic words about the dark side of life, about the possibilities of life: Morrison's songs spoke volumes about his fears and obsessions. Unlike the trippy West Coast rock scene evolving around them, the Doors were always literate – though at their worst they sound verbose and repetitious. It's easy to call Morrison pretentious, but his pretensions were always based on knowledge: he'd done his homework.

His songs also captured a certain side of Los Angeles: the dark, nihilistic side. If his arcane and portentous lyrics were essentially a celebration of his own existence, he also had the ability to focus on the restless nature of West Coast youth. He may have been professionally expedient but he also happened to be in the right place at the right time.

By the autumn of 1966, although he still occasionally looked awkward in performance, Morrison had developed such a strong stage persona that it began to envelop his whole personality. Now, he wasn't just arrogant, enigmatic and resolutely sexual onstage – he was like it offstage, too. Fuelled by huge quantities of acid and beer, he evolved into a sullen erotic showman – the hedonistic poet. Like his hero, Elvis, he had charisma and star quality, things most people couldn't learn. Only Morrison used this raw quality to create his personality.

Having established themselves on the West Coast, in November the Doors flew to New York for their first out-of-town concerts. Since it had opened at the beginning of 1965, Ondine's had been one of the chic-est clubs in Manhattan, and its East 59th Street location was now a Mecca for young, glamorous New Yorkers. It was the very apex of hipness, and it was no surprise that the group decided to make their East Coast debut there. Fortified by their new-found fame, they turned in dynamic performances and took the city by storm. They were a pop-cultural whirlwind.

While in New York Morrison was a frequent visitor to the club, even when the band weren't performing, quickly embroiling himself in the scene. The Doors played at Ondine's again the following spring, the singer treating the club as a second home. His behaviour was becoming predictable: he would drink himself into unconsciousness, often having to be carried home.

Andy Warhol, in *POPism*, remembers it well: 'Jim would stand at the bar drinking screwdrivers all night long, taking down[er]s with them, and he'd get really far gone – he'd be totally oblivious – and the girls would go over and jerk him off while he was standing there.'

Warhol also pinpointed part of Morrison's appeal: 'It was obvious just from watching these kids operate that there were new sex-manoeuver codes. The girls were only interested in the guys that didn't go after them. I saw a lot of girls pass on Warren Beatty, who was so good looking, just because they knew he wanted to fuck them, and they'd go looking for somebody who looked like he didn't want to, who had "problems".'

Morrison had agreed to be the star of Warhol's first blue movie, but when the time came he didn't show up. The following summer he was also meant to appear in another Warhol movie, *I, a Man*, with Nico, but again the proposed collaboration came to nothing.

It was in New York that Morrison first met Danny Fields, the Elektra press agent who would work with the band for most of their career. 'When I first met him,' said Fields, 'I thought he was intriguing, but sullen. At the time I pretty much thought he was another singer – a bit shifty, a little difficult, a little stubborn, but another singer. But after spending time with him I knew he was different, I knew he'd be trouble. Very quickly his character began to take shape. I realised he wasn't very nice – he wasn't very warm, he wasn't very giving, and he began adopting the persona he invented for the stage – you know, dark, brooding, mysterious. That's when he became an asshole.'

At one of the soundchecks at Ondine's, Steve Harris, the Vice President of Elektra, also had his first glimpse of the star: 'He sauntered over to me from the bar – where else – and I thought to myself, if this guy can recite the phone book, he's going to sell a million records. He had a way of moving, a way of looking at you, and a way of projecting himself; he was gorgeous, magnetic. He knew he had the goods, and he knew how to use them. He was very clever, and though he was often a slob, whenever he was introduced to a journalist or a record-company person at a party or whatever, and they had their wife with them, he would always try and conquer the wife first. And he usually did. I know he grew to hate the sex-symbol thing, but at the beginning he was always after the adoration. And he unified that image onstage, and off.'

It was during their first stint at Ondine's that Morrison's mother tried to contact him. After getting through to Steve Harris, and finding out where he was staying, she called Morrison direct, at the Henry Hudson Hotel on West 57th Street. Morrison talked briefly with her on the phone, and then went off in a tantrum. In the years to come members of his family, usually his mother or brother, would try to get in touch with him, more often than not to little or no avail, Morrison refusing to speak to them and then going off in a rage, often to get blind drunk. The old life was behind him now, and he didn't want his family interfering with his new personality. He had reinvented himself, and there was no going back.

This new image enveloped Morrison completely. Immediately after a particularly successful concert at the Fillmore West early in 1967, the singer took Steve Harris aside and asked him if he thought it would be a good publicity stunt if Morrison disappeared, and Elektra started a death hoax. 'It's a good idea,' said Harris, 'but there's just one problem. No one knows who you are yet.'

The Doors remains one of the most extraordinary debut albums in rock history, as influential now as it was when it was released. This was no confused rock and roll arrangement – it was a statement of intent. Released in January 1967, the group's first LP established a powerful and theatrical rock-blues style, and was a blueprint for their whole career.

The album was produced, as were all subsequent records apart from *LA Woman*, by Paul Rothchild, a thirty-year-old fan of the band who had just finished an eight-month jail sentence for smuggling marijuana. Assigned to the group by Elektra – Jac Holzman had the producer flown in from New York – Rothchild immediately clicked with them, becoming almost a fifth member. He understood what they were trying to do, and had a sympathetic ear. He got them to record in Sunset Sound, a studio renowned for its 'live' feel, something which made the band sound all the more assertive. Most of the LP was recorded quickly as the band had played the songs so many times, and rehearsals weren't necessary. Recorded live, nearly everything was cut in a couple of takes. A bass player was drafted in to beef up Manzarek's tinny Fender keyboard bass on a few songs, but the resulting record was practically an exact copy of the Doors' stage sound.

The sound of this first Doors record was remarkable for a variety of reasons: not only for the great tunes or for the sophistication of the lyrics, but for the crystal-clear definition – it sounded *clean*. Because this was his first time in a proper recording studio, Morrison was mostly well behaved, and his enthusiasm for the project manifested itself in his extraordinary perform-ances. He knew this was his chance of immortality; he was, to quote one journalist, 'conscious of the Kleig lights monitoring his every move'. Recording was occasionally postponed when he came in too drunk to sing (or when he didn't turn up at all), but mostly it went according to plan.

And what a plan it was. A blueprint for a dark new tomorrow, *The Doors* was full of haunting little trailers of the future, compelling tales of transcendence, sexu-ality, death and, in Morrison's own words, 'celebrations of existence'. These topics were hardly standard pop fare, and in a world dominated by the Monkees, the Box Tops and the Turtles, the Doors stuck out like a sore thumb, all swollen and bleeding. These sensuous, acid-induced songs were quite unlike anything that had been heard before – modern life as synthesised by an egotistical 'shaman' in leather trousers. Morrison's songs were clipped little poems which he turned into rock and roll vignettes – urgent, obsessive songs of freedom and spiritual death – what he called 'a journey into truth'.

Most of Morrison's early songs share a similar refrain: forget your past and create your future: 'break on through', 'learn to forget', travel to the 'end of the night'.

But if Morrison's lyrics were full of rich imagery and cryptic trivia, the songs themselves were carefully constructed pop packages. Manzarek, Krieger and Densmore created a whirlwind of a backdrop, a gorgeous, malevolent swirl of sounds which evoked the dread side of flower power: sly, hypnotic blues – electric white man's blues. 'Break On Through', 'The Crystal Ship', 'End of the Night' and the rest are figments of Morrison's imagination, sung in his rugged, flat baritone, and bathed in Manzarek's surreal, phantom fairground organ, that distinctive Baroque hurdy-gurdy sound which characterised all their best records. Among Morrison's life-or-death snapshots were a couple of dazzling cover versions: Kurt Weill and Bertolt Brecht's 'Alabama Song (Whisky Bar)' and Willie Dixon's 'Back Door Man' – avant-garde pomp and deep, dark blues. The Monkees they most certainly weren't.

'The End', an eleven-and-a-half-minute epic in which Morrison spelt out his existential theories, closed side two – a sprawling, bombastic poem, it became the band's anthem. If 'Light My Fire' identified them as a *Billboard* pop band, 'The End' cast them as art terrorists. It bordered on the pretentious – Morrison taking his 'ring out the old, ring in the new' theme to extremes – yet somehow the band got away with it. When they recorded it, they had only performed that version (complete with the Oedipal section, where Morrison expresses his desire to fuck his mother and kill his father) once before. As Paul Rothchild said, '"The End" was an always-changing piece. Jim tended to use it as a kind of open, almost blank canvas for his poetic bits and pieces, images and fragments, couplets and the little things he just wanted to say, and it changed all the time . . . After it was down on record, they could listen to it and tended to perform it that way, but Jim still used to leave something out, put something else in, transpose verses.'

In July 1967 a much-abridged version of 'Light My Fire' was released as a single. It quickly climbed the American charts, staying at number one for three weeks and selling over a million copies, becoming the biggest selling single of the year in the process. (The first single from the LP, 'Break On Through', had previously sunk without trace.) Written by Robby Krieger, it would become their best-selling single, and it remains their best-known song. 'In order to compete with Jim's songs, I knew I'd have to be pretty good,' said Krieger in 1988. 'I figured I'd keep it on a universal scale and write about earth, air, fire or water. I picked fire, mainly because I always liked that song by the Stones, "Play With Fire".'

In his best Elvis Presley voice, Morrison poured heart and soul into the song, sending out an invitation to all the young girls in the world. 'Jim had this idea of the band being like a shooting star, going up real fast and being a huge success,' said Krieger. 'For him, it was too slow in happening, even when "Light My Fire" hit. But without it, we probably would never have stayed together.'

But they did, basking in the attention the song's success brought them. Overnight, like all good pop sensations, the Doors became a little larger than life itself.

The Doors was greeted with open arms by the world's rock press, given rave reviews by all the critics who counted. There were those who didn't understand what the band were doing, but they only helped to fan the flames surrounding their success. To the press, who quickly realised that the Doors revolved around the lead singer, Morrison was a godsend – a handsome, articulate, intelligent rock singer increasingly capable of giving good copy. Morrison was never lost for words, and always provided journalists with sufficient quotes.

He knew which journalists worked for which papers, and he tailored his interviews accordingly, always coming up with the goods.

'He proved quite early on that he was his own master manipulator,' said Danny Fields. 'I don't think there was anything, any magazine, he didn't get [coverage in]. He never asked, where is this coming from, how am I getting this, I want more. He gave the journalists what they wanted, and he got what he wanted in return. He did seem in many ways that he was a thousand years old, in his cunning, and his ways to control people . . . even though he acted like an adolescent. But because he was so calculating, and manipulative, he wasn't the kind of guy you'd want to know. He'd hang out with people for a while, but he had no real friends.'

In the Elektra press release which accompanied the release of the album, Morrison set out his own personal manifesto, the first of many. 'You could say it's an accident that I was ideally suited for the work I am doing. It's the feeling of a bowstring being pulled back for twenty-two years and suddenly being let go. I've always been attracted to ideas that were about revolt against authority. I like ideas about the breaking away or overthrowing of established order. I am interested in anything about revolt, disorder, chaos – especially activity that seems to have no meaning. It seems to me to be the road toward freedom – external revolt is a way to bring about internal freedom. Rather than starting inside, I start outside – reach the mental through the physical.'

He also stated that his parents, his whole family, were dead. As far as Morrison was concerned, it was true. In his head he was now the Lizard King, and Lizard Kings weren't meant to have parents.

It wasn't just Morrison, though, who resorted to subterfuge. Soon after the album's release, Steve Harris hired a small group of girls – 'girls who would get their arms cut off on the subway for Jim Morrison' – to follow the band around and create as much hysteria as they could while they were on tour. Through an intricate network of contacts, these girls made sure there were gangs of other girls parked outside the band's dressing rooms and hotel rooms, that there was screaming at the concerts, and that flowers and underwear got thrown onstage. Similar schemes had been devised for Elvis, Frank Sinatra and the Beatles, and while it was a fail-safe trick to guarantee press attention, the acts in any case quickly found a huge audience of genuine fans. The Doors were also the first rock group to use a bill-board to promote their product – above a clothes shop called Pandora's Box on Sunset Boulevard. 'The Doors break on through with an electrifying new album,' it screamed.

As the album continued to sell in vast quantities (*The Doors* would stay in the charts for two years) and as the group performed in Los Angeles, San Francisco and

New York, Morrison's public image was confirmed. Intense and assured, he was a new rock hero with hooded Garbo eyes and a sexy Southern drawl. But in private he was already beginning to disintegrate. He had finally moved in to Pamela Courson's apartment in Laurel Canyon, but continued his philandering; and his drinking was starting to become such a problem that the group began hiring 'babysitters' to look after him. The Doors were getting more famous, playing bigger theatres to bigger audiences, and their entourage grew to include an array of managers, lawyers and publicists. Their records were selling all over the world, and their pictures were in all the right magazines. Yet at its very core their world was already falling apart.

3

Dressing Up for Strange Days

Looking the way he did, being born
that way, was not entirely terrible
Grace Slick, Jefferson Airplane

Morrison was born lucky. If adolescence had briefly tarnished his image with a layer of puppy fat, by the time he wanted to become a rock star his looks were second to none. He had height, a good physique, and the right profile. If you look at the first publicity pictures of the Doors, Morrison looks ungainly and unremarkable in his Haight-Ashbury rags and Carnaby Street chic; but undress him with your eyes and you see a surf-born Adonis. He had the raw material – all he had to do was create a uniform that matched the group's dark urban soundtrack. He had created his own psychic cocktail, his own mythology (a mish-mash of Nietzsche, French theatre, Greek symbolism, contemporary psychology and silly hippie rhetoric). Now his outward appearance needed the same juxtaposition of forces. Like Elvis, he created his look from a variety of sources, clothes which were fundamental to the creation of the Lizard King's image.

To celebrate 'Light My Fire' reaching number one in the charts, Morrison went out and bought his most iconic piece of clothing, a custom-made black leather suit. But the image wasn't all his. In May 1966, Morrison had seen the Velvet Underground perform at the Trip on Sunset Strip; in the audience was Gerard Malanga, a Factory stalwart (and later the Velvets' biographer), dressed from head to toe in tight, black leather. Malanga's outfit that night had a huge effect on Morrison, who quickly realised that to make any kind of lasting impression on the West Coast crowd he'd have to adapt the East Coast chic of the bohemian New Yorkers.

Morrison's leather trousers were not only tailor-made – they were made out of kid-glove leather, which is thinner, finer and far more delicate. At first the tailor thought Morrison had made a mistake and so refused to make them, but he quickly realised that the singer didn't want them any other way. He also asked for them to be cut in the same style as his Levi's, which were narrower than most leather trousers.

'They were super; they just fit,' said Ray Manzarek, who was with Morrison when he went to pick them up. 'They were like snakeskin. He looked like a snake, man. He looked like a black mamba. He put on those leather pants and from the waist down he had turned into a black mamba. That was the beginning of the reign of Jim Morrison the sex symbol, Jim Morrison the sex idol onstage, when he became the black mamba. That was it, man, it was all over. All the women who saw him just absolutely fell in love.'

His cheeks were already gaunt, his torso was lean, and he had those cheekbones, pectorals and wraparound sunglasses – but it took a top Hollywood hair stylist to give him the Alexander the Great haircut he craved. Now the Young Lion added an American-Indian concha belt, cowboy boots and a black gangster hat (complete with a metal skull-and-crossbones motif), all of which he wore with a complete lack of irony. He also bought a solid-gold microphone which he liked to carry from gig to gig. His clothes, like his lyrics, were full of allusion and metaphor – chic, uncompromising and sexy.

Today it is commonplace for pop stars to use their music as a vehicle for indulging their ego. The last five decades have seen pop music become an open prison for the maladjusted, a home for so many appalling egos, all signed up by record companies in the hope that some of their warped genius will transmute into dollars. But Morrison was one of the first to seriously abuse the medium.

Apart from Dionysus, another obsession of Morrison's was, to quote Mick Farren, who wrote about him in *The Black Leather Jacket*, 'the kind of ancient fertility religions that ensured their followers' survival and prosperity by choosing a monarch (usually young, cute, male and virile), who would be sacrificed (usually by young, cute, nubile females) after seven years or some other suitable mystic period. Morrison's writing makes it clear that this was the role he wanted, if not for his total being, then certainly for his stage persona.'

In his eyes he was a victim, dressed in black leather. He proposed himself explicitly as his generation's sacrificial lamb: 'We are obsessed with heroes who live for us and whom we punish.' As Farren pointed out, this wasn't merely a bleak observation: it was Morrison's job description and career goal. Dressed in his martyr's garb, he was ready to be lauded, victimised, reviled and immortalised. He would grow to hate this self-conscious beefcake image – it was only studied perversity, after all – but it was all his own creation. By covering himself with this reptile skin, Morrison gave himself a mask, but he knew if he ever took it off, he would be in deep trouble.

'He was the Lizard King and he could do anything,' said Farren. 'That theoretically included the ability to shed his skin at the crucial moment and slip away before they could stretch him out on the altar and reach for the knife. (It's quite possible that the guilt for this cosmic deceit would have been enough on its own to force him to drink himself to death.)'

The sartorial symbolism of the leather worked on many different levels: 'Morrison had clearly given a good deal of thought to the psycho/sex/freako trappings which go with a leather suit,' said Farren. 'Without doubt, he had evolved the kind of long, complex, floating theory that's the delight of the continuously loaded. Anyone who goes around calling himself the Lizard King is virtually compelled to take what might be called the reptile route. The reptile route is a loose cocktail of Jungian phallic symbolism and dinosaur fear – all that Carl Sagan stuff about how we all have this generic memory from the time when dinosaurs not only ruled the earth but all liked to snack on our ancestors, the first cuddly little mammals. This comes out of the cerebral blender as the explanation that, when you dress up in black leather, you've given yourself the approximation of a shiny reptile skin. When you confront other humans, they're filled with an echo of the fear felt by an early cuddly mammal faced with a hungry and carnivorous dinosaur. It's tortuous even for a pervert.'

Morrison's image was so iconic it was even copied by Presley himself. For the King's 1968 comeback TV special, costume designer Bill Belew fashioned a black leather costume for Elvis, almost entirely based on Morrison's. It not only resurrected Presley's career, but also re-established him as a sex symbol.

Because he carried his life around in a plastic bag (sleeping in a different hotel every night, often keeping his clothes in the trunk of his car), Morrison had permanent body odour.

Danny Fields remembered that, 'He never changed his clothes. Once he had a brand new snakeskin suit, and he walked into the Elektra reception and everyone was amazed to see him in something different. Someone asked him where the snake was, and Jim said "Inside". He loved that lizard metaphor. He owned nothing, that was part of his make-up. He could always escape, change hotels or leave town, switch girls.'

He was purposeful about his anonymity, never wanting to be tied down to anyone or anything; feeling that his life was becoming trapped inside a badly scripted movie, the tormented hedonist found it easy to wander from scene to scene with scant regard for reality.

His perpetual drunkenness also made it easier for him to sleep his way around Hollywood. There are hundreds of Jim Morrison sex stories: tales of impotence, violence, remarkable prowess and appalling degradation. There are also other less sensational stories.

Pamela Des Barres, the once-notorious rock groupie with whom Morrison had a less-than-torrid affair during 1967, spoke of a quiet man, with an occasional temper. She enjoyed being with the singer, going to parties, walking along the shore, taking drugs (an early form of liquid 'angel dust' was an occasional favourite), but mostly just necking.

'In those days you could tell someone you didn't want to get fucked and they'd respect it. Jim did. We went to third base, but he understood that I didn't want to go any further. When I first met him he was a sweety – very quiet and very shy offstage. He was very caring. He never talked about his work with the Doors, just about his poetry. He used to carry it around with him all the time. He was so sweet . . . he was like a poet. But a year later I met him in the Whisky and he slapped my face and threw a bottle of beer at a friend of mine. He'd lost it, it was too bad, but he lost it completely. The thing was, at that time no one really knew how far you could push things – everyone was taking the most incredible amount of drugs – and no one really knew when to stop. But Jim got an addiction, and that was that . . .'

'He wasn't as promiscuous as people say he was,' said Danny Fields, 'and tended to hang on to one woman at a time. He let himself be attacked by girls, he was sort of passively promiscuous. If some piece of trash came up and sat on his cock, he wouldn't pick her up and throw her off. But he didn't go out with the specific intention of picking girls up – and he certainly didn't order people to get him girls. If they came and conquered him, that was fine. His life was a series of rather long relationships, and he always had a woman somewhere. He didn't have a girl every night, but he didn't push them away, either. I don't think he loved to fuck.'

There will always be rumours, but there is little to suggest that Morrison was in any way gay. In *Rock Dreams*, the 1973 picture book written by Nik Cohn and illustrated by Guy Peellaert, a pouting, muscular Morrison is depicted as a gay icon, a leather queen in tight black pants and a string vest. In a crowded bar he perches on a stool, surrounded by rent boys, sailors and drag queens, in a scene reminiscent of the photograph on the gatefold sleeve of *Morrison Hotel*. Standing behind him is Roy Orbison, one of the original leather boys. Nik Cohn said this was an obvious portrait of Morrison, if a little perverse: 'At the time he was so much the most beautiful boy in the world. He was the ultimate idol, for girls and boys alike. But he wasn't drawn that way [by Peellaert] because of his personal habits.'

'I think he found it uncomfortable being adored by men, because he was so sexy,' said Danny Fields. 'On the other hand, he would have complained if it had stopped.'

Writing only two years after Morrison's death, Cohn already had a handle on his enduring success: 'At first Morrison seemed no more than a marvellous boy in black leathers, made up by two queens on the phone. Later on, however, he emerged as something altogether more solemn. Not just a truck-stop rocker, nor even a golden stud, but a poet and a thinker, stuff full of profundities. Forthwith he embarked, like a rock and roll Bix Beiderbecke, full speed ahead on the American route to romantic martyrdom.'

Jim Morrison was instant myth.

By now Morrison was turning into a furious and indiscriminate drinker. He liked alcohol because it fitted in with his particular slant on the Dionysian myth – getting drunk and picking up (or being picked up by) women. His macho code was also influenced by Norman Mailer, and his chosen drug, alcohol, helped him to see this through. By drinking beer (or anything else) he didn't have to rely on anyone – no sycophantic dealers or wealthy women: he could walk into any bar and get his prescription, right there and then. 'I hate the kind of sleazy sexual connotations of scoring from people,' he said, 'so I never do that. That's why I like alcohol; you can go down to any corner store or bar and it's right across the table . . . It's traditional.'

'It's like gambling somehow,' he said another time. 'You go out for a night of drinking and you don't know where you're going to end up the next day. It could work out good or it could be disastrous. It's like the throw of the dice.'

Morrison liked places that were noisy and beery and cloudy with grease. He wouldn't have known how to behave in anywhere smart, not that anywhere smart would have tolerated his behaviour. The singer wasn't born feral, but that's what he had become. He would be so drunk he listed, swaying from side to side until he staggered back to wherever it was he was staying, his face covered in crazyhouse drool.

Odds on, his nights turned out disastrously. Slumped over a wipe-clean bar, he'd drink himself paralytic, maybe forcing a fellow drunk into a long philosophical discussion, perhaps reading his poetry, or trying to pick up a passing waitress or stripper, and then throwing the inevitable bottle or chair before being thrown out. Morrison was the ultimate barstool philosopher.

The days could be disastrous, too. Once, on a shopping spree in LA, he walked into a jeans store to buy some leather trousers. Completely drunk, he undressed and asked for a pair which were way too small for him. He hardly ever wore underwear and stood there half naked while the assistant tried to persuade him to get dressed. He didn't, but just demanded to see more jeans. He tried on a pair with lace-up flies, but was so far gone he had to ask the assistant to tie them for him. He liked the trousers, but paid the assistant $500 to replace the fly with a zip, even though there was an identical pair with a zip on the rail behind him.

Pop genius but amateur human being, Morrison was already losing his equilibrium. While he was starting to be seen as a rock god, his real life couldn't quite live up to the myth.

There were other nights: on 3 August 1966, the night Lenny Bruce died, David Crosby was, for no apparent reason, attacked by Morrison at the Whisky a Go Go in Los Angeles. He harangued Crosby, and accused him of hiding behind his sunglasses, though Crosby was wearing shades only because he was strung out on acid. This behaviour was typical: in his autobiography *Long Time Gone*, Crosby remembered Morrison as having 'a masochistic bent; he sublimated it. He'd go out and get monumentally trashed – drunk, high, and really polluted – and pick a fight with someone who would beat him up. He did it repeatedly.'

Crosby remembered a party where Morrison got into a fight with Janis Joplin: 'Jim tells Janis she can't sing the blues, which does not make her happy. Her first reaction was to run out of the room, crying. Then, being the spunky bluesy bitch she was, Janis picked up a bottle of Jim Beam bourbon (the square one with the sharp corners) and, instead of taking a drink, took the bottle back into the room with Morrison, where she broke it on his forehead.

'Jim went down onto the rug, but not completely out of it. He had enough consciousness left to puke into the shag carpet around his face.'

Jim Morrison found it easy being a star. Easy for him, difficult for everyone else; everyone, that is, with whom he came into contact. Both in public and in private, he could treat those around him with unbridled contempt. He would push relationships – with friends, lovers and fans – to the brink, just to watch them break. He wanted to see just how far he could go. But the success of the Doors had been so quick, his fame so accelerated, that he soon became appalled at how easy all this was, and was especially disgusted with the public's seemingly unrelenting masochism. He pushed his 'live performance' self to the limit, insulting and assaulting the audience, only to have them love him in return. He realised he could push himself even further than he originally thought, so his already highly theatrical persona quickly descended into self-parody.

Almost from their first success, Morrison acknowledged the limitations of the Doors; he was not content, like Manzarek, Krieger and Densmore, to sit back and ride the gravy train.

He became taciturn and difficult, sometimes even violent. Onstage he would throw lighted cigarettes into the audience, and jump into the pit to chastise fans; he would try to scare them by suddenly stopping singing halfway through a song, only to stare at them with his smug grin, defiant in his silence. At parties he would throw ice cubes and bottles at girls who annoyed or ignored him. He was playing the tortured artist now, the frustrated phantom. It was impossible to get him to do anything he didn't want to. When the band appeared on *The Ed Sullivan Show* on 17 September 1967, Sullivan asked them to omit the word 'higher' from 'Light My Fire'. Morrison agreed, but then sang it anyway.

Night after night he trundled from bar to bar along Sunset Strip, sometimes picking up a girl, sometimes befriending a group of drunks before stripping naked in the street and maybe scaling a hotel wall, or playing the matador with cars on the freeway. And he slept where he fell. God help anyone who tried to help him.

'You never went to criticise Jim face-to-face,' said Danny Fields, 'you just didn't do it. Paul [Rothchild] would obviously order him about in the studio, but I would never say, "Why don't you shave, or lose ten pounds, or use a deodorant?" It never occurred to me, or anyone else. The rest of the band worked around him. I never saw anyone treat him like anyone but Elvis Presley.'

But Fields had quickly fallen out with Morrison, who resented the press officer's attempts to help his career . . . as well as saving his life. This happened in July 1967, when Fields had, in Morrison's eyes, tried to kidnap him. Distressed by the kind of girls Morrison was surrounding himself with (mainly down-at-heel circuit groupies), Fields tried to elevate his taste in women – firstly by introducing him to Nico, the former model and chanteuse with the Velvet Underground, the East Coast's answer to the Doors. 'I thought they would make a cute couple,' said Fields. 'They were both so weird and icy and mysterious and charismatic and poetic and deep and sensitive and wonderful.'

Nico was in LA staying with Edie Sedgwick, the Warhol girl, at the Castle Hotel in the Hollywood Hills, a huge fake 1920s Spanish mansion which had recently become a popular rock and rollers' haunt, frequented by the likes of Jefferson Airplane, Bob Dylan and Warhol himself. 'I rounded him up and persuaded him to follow me to the Castle in his car,' said Fields. 'You could tell how nasty he was then, because he really wasn't trying to keep up – falling back and being a real pain in the ass – so I'd have to keep stopping and waiting for him. He played those kinds of games, tried to get you in his power. So, we got there, and after I introduced them they just stood and stared at each other for hours. They stood in doorways and stared at the same spot on the floor.

'Then we got incredibly stoned. I travelled with a lot of drugs in those days – everyone did – and we took just about everything I had – everything, that is, that hadn't been taken by Edie Sedgwick. I had hidden most of my drugs underneath the mattress of a bed in a room that wasn't being used, but she still managed to find them. There was acid, hash, uppers, downers, and a bottle of vodka. I split most of this with Jim, although he had far more than I did – he had a much greater capacity for narcotics than anyone I knew. It was amazing. I didn't know how anybody drunk, smoked and swallowed so much stuff and still stayed up. But he did. He was up on the roof, naked, climbing all over it, completely stoned.'

'He took Nico up in a tower, both naked,' said Paul Rothchild, 'and Jim, stoned out of his mind, walked along the edge of the parapet. Hundreds of feet down. Here's this rock star at the peak of his career risking his life to prove to this girl that life is nothing.'

'Him and Nico got into this fight,' said Fields, 'with him pulling her hair all over the place – it was just this weird love-making, between the two most adorable monsters, each one trying to be more poetic than the other. Then he started asking for his car keys, and of course I was afraid that he was so drunk he'd kill himself, so I told him no and hid the keys. The worst situation in the world for him was to be out of control, to be in the thrall of other people. He hated that.'

Morrison snarled and shouted and an argument broke out. Unable to win, he crawled to bed. The next day, still drunk, still drinking, Morrison again begged for his car, which again Fields denied him, eventually agreeing to drive Jim downtown to his own car.

'Whilst we were gone,' said Fields, 'the group had been to the Castle looking for him, because he was due at a rehearsal. When we came back we found all the chairs on the table – this was their way of expressing anger. They were all scared of him, all very, very afraid of him. They loved him, but they hated him as much as they loved him. They knew that he was everything. Before they'd gone they'd written on the back of a still from the *Chelsea Girls* movie which was hanging up in the lobby: "Jim, you'd better get back, your ass is mud."

'A little while later, after he'd sobered up, I put his keys back in the ignition, telling him they were there all the time. He hated me from that moment on. He thought I was being sneaky and treacherous, and I was, but I was also being protective. I didn't care if he got killed, but the record company would have lost their biggest star and I would have lost my job.

'And that one very intense night we spent together, taking all those drugs and talking all night long, it was so incredible. It was a very intense experience, probably the most intense I've ever had. I can't remember what was said, because we were on acid, but you know, it was deep. You'd think that some kind of bond would remain after that, so at least you acknowledge that there had been some kind of intimacy, even if it's embarrassing for you to recall, but he never did. It's like if you slept with someone once, as much as you don't want to say anything about it, or nudge or wink or whatever, something is always there. Not that we slept together . . . but it was so close.'

Nico later dyed her hair because she'd heard that Morrison liked redheads: 'I was so in love with him that I made my hair red after a while. I wanted to please his taste. It was silly, wasn't it? Like a teenager.'

As Danny Fields said, 'It wasn't a gratifying experience working for Morrison, it was always kinda frustrating. He never really did what I wanted, but I was naive too – it was my first job as a legitimate publicist and people don't do what you want them to do. He had his own idea of how he wanted his image projected, and he was right. He was the custodian of his own creation. I flattered myself that I could manipulate it, but he was a much better manipulator than anyone.

'I wanted him to do a photo session with Nico, but he refused to do it. He'd never say no, but he'd never turn up. Nico would be waiting at the location and Morrison was always nowhere to be seen. He didn't want to pose with a woman, and I don't blame him – his instincts were right. Posing with a woman would have diffused his image, and he wanted to remain aloof.'

Fields had other plans for the group, figuring that they should broaden their popularity by exploiting the teen market, a huge portion of which was buying the Doors' records anyway. He wanted to introduce Morrison – whom he saw as the archetypal new-wave teen icon – to Gloria Stavers, the editor of *16* magazine. Fields flew from New York to Los Angeles with the express purpose of getting Morrison to place a call to her.

Stavers was a powerful woman at the time, controlling the hearts and minds of nearly every fourteen-year-old girl in America, and she asked for and received a great deal of deference from the music industry. Morrison, though, was hardly the kind of fawning pop star she was used to. She consequently became intrigued by, and then obsessed with, the singer.

Fields' ruse worked, and not only did Morrison and Stavers become lovers, but he became a visible inhabitant of *16*, extending his career substantially. Predictably, though, Morrison treated her badly. Once he had a date with her in New York: after arriving at the Chelsea Hotel from LA, he called her up and invited her over. They hadn't seen each other for a while, and Gloria was tremendously excited, so she rushed down to the hotel. Though she was tough and terse in business, she could be like a little girl when she was in love.

When she got to his room, the door was open so she went in. She looked for him, called out his name, but he was nowhere to be seen. She called his name for over fifteen minutes and then left. When she got back to her apartment the phone was ringing. It was Morrison. 'Where are you?' she asked.

'In my room,' he said.

'I was just there,' Gloria explained, 'and I looked everywhere for you ...'

'Not under the bed,' he said.

Morrison was full of silly little tricks. Rothchild and Fields took him to dinner once in LA, and he didn't say a word all night, pointing at things he wanted on the menu. Even when they insulted him, he just stared at his food, gulping down huge quantities of wine and belching when appropriate. For America's biggest pop star, being difficult was the easiest thing in the world.

By the time of their second LP, *Strange Days*, released in November 1967, the Doors were as big as the Beatles and, in the eyes of the press, twice as subversive. Treated with reverence by their fans and with muted respect by the establishment, the band were beyond criticism, and all they had to do was consolidate that position.

Strange Days certainly didn't rock the boat, being a virtual photocopy of their debut, a madcap medley of discontent, with plenty of gothic orchestration. But if their first record had been an invitation to glimpse the dark side of life, *Strange Days* was a guided tour. The sex and death motifs were still in abundance, as were the quirky little love songs and the apocalyptic overtures. The record may have been portentous and melodramatic, but it had great tunes. 'People Are Strange' is perhaps the finest piece of post-acid paranoia ever recorded. With this track the Doors captured that sense of what happened *after* drugs: when acid really hit Los Angeles, the Doors' music was the most appropriate soundtrack, as it spoke to those people who were *really* changing their lives with drugs. Their music captured too the sleaze and furtiveness of the times. The Beach Boys and the Doors spoke for two different sides of Los Angeles, and in 1967 it was the Doors who were talking the loudest. This was the end of an endless summer. Morrison always felt there was something deeply disturbing and bogus about the so-called Summer of Love (to his credit, Jefferson Airplane's Paul Kantner said that the Summer of Love should have simply been called the golden age of fucking), and he used this theme like a mantra in his songs. On *Strange Days*, with its eerie underwater organ sound, backward tapes and lethargic tone, he sounds like a drugged beast stalking through paradise.

'I offer images,' Morrison said at the time. 'I conjure memories of freedom that can still be reached – like the Doors, right? But we can only open the doors – we can't drag people through. I can't free them unless they want to be free … A person has to be willing to give up everything, not just wealth. All the bullshit he's been taught, all society's brainwashing. You have to let go of all that to get to the other side. Most people aren't willing to do that.'

The only tell-tale sign of things to come was the opus that ended side two: 'When the Music's Over'. A distillation of everything on their first LP – the magical significance of rock music, alienation, nihilism, doomed romance – it seemed somewhat forced in its evocation of Armageddon (in one apocalyptic outburst he asks for his subscription to the resurrection to be cancelled). As in a lot of his songs, here Morrison was orchestrating his own funeral. Detached, mysterious and allusive, Morrison's obsessive and allegorical lyrics (mostly concerning his unrelenting death wish) were as haunting as they had been on the first album.

The Doors was recorded on 4-track, but after its release the Sunset Sound Studio was converted to 8-track. That was when, according to Manzarek, 'We began to experiment with the studio itself, as an instrument to be played. Those eight tracks to us were really liberating. So at that point we began to play ... it became five people: keyboards, drums, guitar, vocalist and studio.' There was another addition to the line-up, as Pamela Courson became a frequent visitor to the studio. Her only contribution, though, occurred during the recording of 'You're Lost, Little Girl' when Paul Rothchild tried to incorporate her into the song by asking her to perform oral sex on Morrison while he recorded the vocal. Not surprisingly, this didn't work, and the song had to be recorded again.

And though Morrison was already going through the motions, he still believed his music could radically help change people's lives, and still talked opportunistically of his shamanistic qualities: 'I think people resist freedom because they're afraid of the unknown. But it's ironic. That unknown was once very well known. It's where our souls belong. The only solution is to confront yourself with the greatest fear imaginable. After that, fear has no power, and fear of freedom shrinks and vanishes.'

The American public lapped this up and *Strange Days* reached number three in the charts.

Their first album featured their portraits on the cover but the band resolutely refused to have another picture of themselves on this one. So Elektra came up with the idea of photographing some carnival freaks instead.

Morrison was amused, thinking it looked like a still from a Fellini movie: 'I hated the cover of our first album, so for *Strange Days* I said, "I don't want to be on this cover. Put a chick on it or something. Let's have a dandelion, or a design," and because of the title, everyone agreed, 'cause that's where we were at, what was happening. It was right. Originally, I wanted us in a room surrounded by about thirty dogs. Everyone was saying, "What are the dogs for?" And I said that it was symbolic that it spelled God backwards. Finally we ended up leaving it to the art director and the photographer. He came up with some freaks, a typical sideshow thing. It looked European.'

Worried that the band's fans might not immediately identify this new product, Elektra placed full-page ads in the rock press, stating: 'Their second super-album, STRANGE DAYS, is now available. Look for it carefully – because THE DOORS are not exactly on the cover. But they sure as hell are inside.'

4

Dance On Fire

The stage is empty, and bathed in darkness. Below, ten thousand avid Doors fans are screaming their pained, ear-piercing screams. A light hovers, and then John Densmore, Robby Krieger and Ray Manzarek quietly walk onto the stage. They calmly engage their instruments and break into song, the aggressive strains of 'Break On Through' filling the auditorium. Manzarek crouches over his piano, intently pursuing the rhythm, as Densmore pounds his drum kit and Krieger walks around like a sentry, looking, as ever, like someone walking onstage to look for his dog.

The intro seems to last for ever, but then the crowd roars with appreciation as something moves offstage. It's a man: about five feet eleven inches tall, 160 pounds (the booze has taken effect), with long, curly brown hair. He wears leather trousers, a flouncy white cotton shirt, black boots and a large American-Indian belt.

Wearing his familiar studied frown, Jim Morrison glides across the stage towards the microphone. 'Hi,' he says, in his best Brando growl. He looks out at the sea of fans, then down to the stage, then quickly behind to his three comrades, and then he cocks his head, shakes his hair, closes his eyes and opens his mouth – the defiant melodramatic gasps of 'Break On Through' at last filling the night air.

He stares off into the darkness, as a crowd of squirming, sweaty girls peer back from the stalls. He gropes himself and screams, internalising for all to see. He grabs the microphone with one hand, wraps one thin leather leg around the skinny steel stand, and places the other on its base, while rubbing his crotch with his spare hand. He rocks back and forward, gently swaying ... and the girls groan with delight. He stalks the stage, singing, little muscles popping in his throat. He jerks, twists, hopping from one foot to the other, jumping like a frog; but he is stilted, unable to express himself fully with his body, finding it difficult to dance. His psycho-sexual energy manifests itself all the same, his partially erect penis clearly visible through his trousers. The band create their familiar wall of sound as Morrison rolls out his catchphrases: 'Cancel my subscription to the resurrection.' 'We want the world and we want it now.' 'I am the Lizard King, I can do anything ...'

During 'The Unknown Soldier' Morrison enacts the obligatory shooting scene while Krieger holds his guitar like a machine gun, suffering from splenetic fits and dropping to the stage, his suggestive body movements and incendiary lyrics provoking a typically enthusiastic response. But this time he grabs a cigarette from the audience before acting out his death – the little leap and the dramatic, dead-bird fall. He slumps to the floor and folds over like a wind-blown leaf. Then he jumps up again, startled, embarrassed by his own phoney seizure.

When he was onstage Morrison underwent a transformation, bringing the cartoon Lizard King to life. Up in front of his public, his usually composed face managed to express the most emotions, 'a thousand masks of tensions'. Onstage, he tried to act out his life.

His dancing was always ungainly, and he hopped about as though he was summoning the gods, in a rain dance of less than epic proportions. His head bent forward, he would jig around the stage, never actually dancing, always aloof, never becoming part of the music. He set himself up as a healer. All hail Morrison! He is here to cure our ills, to feed our poor and fill our souls. All hail the King! Oh lordy, the drunk King!

And then he'd belch and scour the front row for bottles of wine, possibly bumming a cigarette as well. Morrison pretended to be possessed, acting out images from his lyrics, working the crowd into a frenzy before doing something calculatedly silly and deflating the whole situation. For his fans he embodied physical magnetism and spiritual restlessness, and he never failed to exploit this.

Sometimes he genuinely seemed to enjoy it: he told *Newsweek*'s John Riley in 1967, 'The only time I really open up is onstage. I feel spiritual up there.'

When he believed in himself he saw these shows as a celebration of existence, of pure unbridled joy: an expression of potency. Mick Farren, in *The Hunting of the Lizard King* (an article in the *NME* in 1975), said what Morrison did 'was present a rhetoric and mime that exactly typified the thoughtless, emotive confusion of the sixties youth revolt. Unlike Dylan, he didn't question. He saw no other point of view than that of the Lizard King's narrow perspective. Onstage, for the few moments Morrison had total control, objectivity was suspended. His histrionics, the prowling, the long insolent stares, the lunges at the mike, and the spasmodic twitching leaps, ceased to be absurd.'

Yet these epiphanies were rare, and mostly the performances were only conceits orchestrated to inflame the audience. Morrison was acting, inflicting his persona on the crowd, enacting his primitive ritual. And acting like a bit of a dick. He was never the real Jim Morrison onstage, but then he was no longer the real Jim Morrison offstage, either.

Ray Manzarek, always Morrison's most fervent defender, remained convinced of the singer's integrity: 'Jim's contribution to music was that he was real onstage. He was not a performer, he was not an entertainer, he was not a showman . . . He was possessed by a vision, by a madness, by a rage to live, by an all-consuming fire to . . . make art.'

Perhaps Paul Rothchild was nearer the truth when he said, 'The Doors always tried to be unique, to be different . . . avant-garde. There was a conscious attempt to be new.'

'The Jim Morrison thing started out as an act, but so many people believed it, that he became that,' said Danny Fields. 'They returned to him what they saw, and he started acting out their fantasy. After all, what does it take? What is a shaman? There were no mystical rays coming from heaven, he wasn't surrounded by an aura – it was just a psychological relationship between him and his admirers. It was all a pose, and he became his own invention. He knew he had a special quality – a kind of dangerous, threatening, menacing sexuality that women went berserk over – and he used that to cover up.'

In the band's early days, Morrison had two set pieces which he would incorporate into their live shows: the first was the Oedipal section of 'The End', the second a dive into the audience. He would just let go and dive into the crowd like it was a pool of water, and the audience would catch him and carry him back to the stage. Though the audience quickly began to expect it, and it is now common, back then no rock performer had ever done such a thing. The jump has since been copied by, among others, Iggy Pop, Peter Gabriel and (unsuccessfully) David Bowie.

'The first time I ever saw him do the dive was in Bido Lido's in May 1967,' said Pamela Des Barres, 'a little ditty place which only held about two hundred people. I was sitting way up in a booth and saw it all. Jim was so dynamic, so brave. He was saying "Fuck it" – he pushed it as far as anyone could. He wanted an adverse reaction, he wanted people to be involved with the show, he wanted them to respond. He would just let go and career into the audience, who would eventually put him back onstage. No one had ever seen anything like it, and Jim didn't even consider the consequences. But it was like he turned it on – he put everything he had into performance.

'It was very black, the way he moved. No one, not even Mick Jagger, had been as overtly sexual as Jim was onstage. It was very James Brown – ripping off his clothes an' all. It was filthy.'

In 1971, when asked by Dan Knapp of the *Los Angeles Times* about the sexual overtones of his performance, Morrison said, 'Sometimes they just happen, and sometimes it's just part of the act.'

By this time he had stopped jumping. He was now so famous he was scared what the crowd might do.

A hypnotic figure dressed in black – Gene Vincent with a college degree – he controls the audience from the safety of the stage. The girls are screaming louder now, as he squirms and vamps in his impossibly tight leather trousers, the human phallus about to reach his climax. The group crashes into 'Light My Fire' and the crowd goes berserk. The king of acid-rock hops in front of Manzarek's piano, pumping the air with his fists, his eyes closed, sweat pouring down his shirt. He wanders over to John Densmore and tries to interfere with his kit. Densmore ignores him and looks to Krieger for guidance. Morrison then kneels before Krieger's guitar and simulates fellatio, something that was again copied by David Bowie during his Ziggy Stardust period, when he pretended to give head to his guitarist, Mick Ronson.

'Light My Fire' is cold-blooded and immaculate, Morrison's ad libs and seemingly impromptu scissor kicks only distracting from the gorgeous wall of noise. He makes constant interruptions: during a lull in 'Gloria', he shouts, 'Little girl, how old are you? Little girl, what school do you go to? Little girl, suck my cock?'

During 'The End', his hands covering his face, he laughs to himself behind the microphone, not wanting the crowd to see how silly he thinks it all is. In one of the quieter sections of 'When the Music's Over' – the audience rapt with attention – he belches into the mike, and laughs. What a gas, he thinks to himself. Are the audience really taking this shit seriously?

A lot of Morrison's songs were of course written from a distance, with a deep sense of irony, but this passed a lot of people by. While journalists like Lester Bangs recognised that Morrison occasionally 'realised the implicit absurdity of the rock and roll bête-noire badass pose and parodied, deglamorised it', others took it at face value. In 1970 Morrison told the *Los Angeles Free Press*: 'That piece "Celebration of the Lizard" was kind of an invitation to the dark forces. It's all done tongue in cheek. I don't think people realise that. It's not to be taken seriously. It's like, if you play the villain in a Western, it doesn't mean that that's you. I really don't take that seriously. That's supposed to be *ironic*.'

'Occasionally,' said Mick Farren, 'he would even hold up the [Morrison] image and demonstrate just how hollow it was. This was more often in front of an audience than the press. At a 1969 Madison Square Garden concert he pointed dramatically to one half of the audience.

'"You are life!" He pointed to the other half. "You are death! I straddle the fence – AND MY BALLS HURT."'

At the concert in New Haven, Connecticut, on 9 December 1967, the day after Morrison's twenty-fourth birthday, the Doors witnessed the first major upset of their career. Before the band's performance, Morrison met a girl backstage, and took her into one of the shower rooms. A police officer, clearing the area, caught the couple necking and asked them to break up and move on. When Morrison protested, the cop brought out an aerosol canister of tear gas from behind his back and sprayed them both in the face, as nonchalantly as if he was throwing a bucket of water over a pair of fighting cats. Later that night, as the band were ploughing their way through 'Back Door Man', Morrison told the crowd his version of the story, repeatedly shouting the word 'pig' and talking in a dumb Southern accent, to antagonise the police. But as Morrison told his tale, the house lights went up and the police invaded the stage, arresting the singer for breach of the peace, later adding the charges of indecent and immoral exhibition and resisting arrest. It was ironic that 1967 should finish this way for the band, as the preceding twelve months had been a succession of triumphs. But now they had been conveniently fingered by the establishment.

Morrison was still seeing Pamela Courson, while continuing to sleep around. He'd graze the bars along Sunset Strip, staying most nights at the Cienega Motel in West Hollywood. Rarely sober, he usually had his first beer of the day with breakfast in one of the many restaurants along La Cienega Boulevard. He continued to get into fights, to abuse the rich and the famous at the various celebrity parties which he was invited to, and constantly tried to gatecrash performances by other rock groups, often crawling onto the stage and trying to join in. (Rock biographer Albert Goldman once interpreted Morrison's brush with Jimi Hendrix, at the Scene in New York – the singer rushed onstage and clutched Hendrix's legs – as an attempted blowjob.)

Consciousness became bearable to Morrison only if he was drunk, and he recruited a small posse of fellow drinkers to accompany him on his binges, including the actor Tom Baker and the then-unknown Alice Cooper. Morrison was always a chameleon, and his most popular guise was that of the boozer. Hidden away, behind the blinds of his motel window, he could be tender and reflective; sitting in a bar at three in the afternoon he could be funny and full of camaraderie; he was generous to the extent of squandering his money, and was always willing to help out a friend. But offstage the Lizard King was a man without conscience, a drunk without a will.

The Doors began recording their third album early in 1968, but the recording sessions were constantly disrupted by the gang of groupies and liggers with which Morrison had surrounded himself. He began inviting them along to the studio at all times of the day, much to the annoyance of the rest of the group. His drinking was also increasing, so much so that the band hired Bob Dylan's ex-minder to look after Morrison, ostensibly to direct a documentary about the Doors, but really to make sure Morrison turned up for recording alone. And though the band still tolerated his drunken displays and non-appearances, John Densmore threatened to quit. So did Morrison, though nobody believed him.

The recording took far longer than before, firstly because a lot of the songs were new, and secondly because Morrison found it difficult to perfect his vocals in anything less than ten takes. 'When he was drunk,' said Paul Rothchild, 'it was odds-on you wouldn't get a vocal.'

In April 1968 'The Unknown Soldier', the first single from the new album, reached number 39 in the American charts. The band made their own 'rock theatre' promo film for the song, in which Morrison was 'shot' on the cross, in a bizarre and gauche crucifixion scene which publicly presented him rather pathetically as the Saviour for the 'love generation'.

Morrison had written the song the last time he was in New York. Steve Harris remembered 'being out with Jim and Paul Rothchild one night, and Jim got so drunk we had to take him home. We found a cab and took him back to his hotel on the West Side, took off all his clothes and put him to bed with a waste-paper basket next to the bed because he was retching. I turned to Paul and said, "Look at this,

this is the biggest star in America, just look at him." Just before we left Jim asked us to bring him his leather trousers, which we did. He then took a small piece of paper out of the pocket, on which were written the lyrics to "The Unknown Soldier". He'd written them that night and then gone out and got completely, outrageously drunk. It must have taken a lot out of him.'

In August 'Hello I Love You', a relatively jaunty pop song, became the band's second US number one (for two weeks) and their second million-seller. Short, taut, and unashamedly commercial, it was a dead ringer for the Ray Davies song 'All Day and All of the Night' recorded by the Kinks in 1964. Still, it contained some of Morrison's best lines, where he mixed Billboard logic with brazen irony, and more than a hint of sex. Never again would he be able to fuse light and dark in such a seamless fashion. This was Morrison making timeless, sexy pop, full of wit, pathos and an inimitable sense of urgency.

It was this kind of Doors record – snappy, Spartan – which appealed so much to American Top 40 radio, whose DJs could hear rampant commerciality among the clever-dick arrangements, monotone vocals and lyrics about dead horses, drugs and sleeping with your mother. Other songs on the new LP were similarly arranged, and both 'Love Street' and 'Summer's Almost Gone' displayed that cunning pop sense.

Elsewhere, things were getting sloppy. By the time Morrison, Manzarek, Krieger and Densmore recorded *Waiting for the Sun*, there was no longer the urgent passion in their work. Released in September of 1968, the third album showed the world that the Doors were fallible, just another rock band. And while the collection was shrink-wrapped by Paul Rothchild's by now distinctive production, many of the songs themselves flagged, being either leftovers from Morrison's Venice days, or hastily written studio compositions.

'Not to Touch the Earth' is an excerpt from an abortive recording of one of Morrison's theatrical extravaganzas, 'Celebration of the Lizard', a would-be tour de force in the style of 'The End'. It was originally meant to occupy a whole side of the record, and it's not surprising that Manzarek made sure it wasn't included, for when it eventually surfaced on *Absolutely Live* in 1970, it was mostly unlistenable, a long, rambling stream of consciousness – Morrison's visions of Nietzschean self-glorification clouded by unwieldy lyrics, drink and his perverse ego.

Tongue firmly in cheek, Morrison explained his preoccupation with the scaly reptile: 'The lizard and the snake are equated with the subconscious forces of evil. Even if you've never seen one, a snake seems to embody everything that we fear. It ['Celebration of the Lizard'] is a kind of invitation to dark, evil forces.'

There were amateur dramatics elsewhere on the record – 'Five to One', one of the album's most enigmatic songs, was pure rhetorical agitprop, a political sham best remembered for its opening chorus, containing one of his most enduring catchphrases, 'no one here gets out alive'; though listeners were spared the snippets of poetry he wanted to include between the songs. ('Five to One' was the approximate ratio of whites to blacks in the US, as well as non-pot smokers to pot smokers. It was also a reference to the number of US citizens under twenty-five, while many think it's just a song about masturbation: five fingers and one cock.)

'We Could Be So Good Together', however, was another classic example of the pop music the Doors made so well, harking back to the formulaic structure of the songs on the first two LPs. Surprisingly, it was their only album to go to the top of the American charts, spending four weeks at number one.

Morrison was bored by recording – it had lost its immediacy for him – so he embroiled himself in his other interests: poetry and film.

He decided to make a documentary about the band (eventually called *Feast of Friends*), asking some friends to direct and produce it. He also began making moves to have his poetry published: a motley collection of half-formed ideas, notes and lyrics he hadn't been able to incorporate into his songs. He saw his future as a poet, blind to the fact that his words lost their importance without the music. On paper they were preposterous and bombastic schoolboy scribblings. Much of Morrison's poetry evoked pain, death, alienation and sex, and drew on Freudian symbolism – all the elements that made the group's songs so powerful. With the Doors he managed to evoke strange and forceful images; with his poetry he provoked embarrassment. On paper his nightmares didn't look real. Nevertheless, there were enough sycophants willing to massage Morrison's ego, and he was encouraged to publish his work. Simon and Schuster would later publish the two collections, *The Lords* and *The New Creatures*, though for now he was content to publish them himself. If the Doors were less of an ensemble and more of a straightforward rock group than Morrison desired, then he would have to explore those other areas alone. The group were more popular than ever, and continued to tour. On 10 May 1968, Morrison incited his first riot, at a Doors performance in Chicago. His contempt for the audience had grown so much that he openly provoked them, causing them to run amok.

Following the release of *Waiting for the Sun*, the Singer Bowl concert in New York also proved difficult. Danny Fields said, 'This was when he started to self-destruct. And he did it in public, turning the audience against him. The Who opened for the Doors that night – there was a nasty crowd, bad security, a disaster waiting to happen. I told him before he went on, "Be careful, Jim, I've a feeling something's going to happen." And he turned to me and said, "How would *you* know?" So he went out there and abused the crowd. That night there was riot number two.'

The Doors were rapidly becoming a freak show. According to Ray Manzarek, 'After the New Haven bust, the vice squad would come. People would come to see this sex god, and to see what he was up to. Then people came to see him expose himself. Then, he freaked out, and they came to see him freak out, even though his freaking out was not really a normal part of the act. They had a love/hate thing for him. They were jealous of him.'

In Britain, by the summer of 1968, the group had become a creature of fiction. They were so different from anything else coming out of America at that time that an aura had built up around them. Their records were difficult to buy and hardly ever played on the radio, and, with the British pop press being somewhat old-fashioned, news of the band's activities seldom crossed the Atlantic. However, one item did manage to find its way into the papers, predictably causing havoc among the Doors' British fans: news of the band's first European tour. They were to co-headline with Jefferson Airplane, in London, Amsterdam, Copenhagen, Stockholm and Frankfurt.

A staggering amount of hype preceded the tour, particularly concerning the group's four proposed concerts at the Roundhouse in North London, during September. Granada TV were planning a TV special called *The Doors Are Open*, and John Peel, fast becoming the country's foremost alternative DJ, was plugging the band and their gigs on his radio show. 'I remember various people slagging them off before they'd even arrived, so I started repeating "Stand clear of the Doors, it can be dangerous to obstruct the Doors," just like they say on the tube trains.'

By this time the British underground saw the Doors as the new Rolling Stones. People thought the concerts would be transcendental, like the records. Needless to say, they failed to live up to such high expectations.

The afternoon before the first concert Morrison was typically quiet backstage. He was on strange turf, so the screens had come up.

This was Morrison the Singular Man, a publicly private man. He was all charm and deference, handshakes and kisses, seemingly happy to mingle with the Roundhouse gofers and groupies. Jeff Dexter, the DJ at the Roundhouse concerts, remembered it well: 'Backstage he got a lot of attention, and he seemed to play along with everyone. But you could tell he wasn't like that. It just looked like an act to me.'

Then, come showtime, fired up by booze (he had foregone the soundcheck in favour of a lone drinking session), knowing that the television crew were filming the event, Morrison slipped into his lizard suit and began his evening ritual, the evocation of the spirits of the American West. He moved like a cripple, swigging on a bottle of Jack Daniel's like a gunfighter, draping himself over the microphone while staring wide-eyed at the stage. His drunk, jerky movements made him look silly, but Morrison was oblivious to it all. The boozy slut in leather pants was in full flight, and if the audience didn't like his act, then to hell with them.

The first concert produced a very hip crowd, the self-appointed gurus of the underground bumping up against a motley collection of trendy students and a battalion of young girls. They blew bubbles and waved their hands in the air; they swapped drugs and admired each other's garb. Chris Rowley, then a stalwart of the underground press, remembered 'there was a lot of leather'.

Jeff Dexter was one of the many dissatisfied punters: 'The Jefferson Airplane played long improvised jams, whereas the Doors stuck to the songs as you heard them on the records, with a few instrumental breaks and a little orchestrated poetry thrown in. This led people to think they were pedestrian. I thought they were just like a pop band, really.'

This was much more of a pop show than a subcultural tour de force, and the Roundhouse crowd saw the Doors for what they were: pure theatre.

Journalist Neil Spencer was in the audience that night. 'I remember being very disappointed that he couldn't dance, and he kept falling about all over the place. At other times the show was so choreographed it didn't look real . . . it looked completely theatrical. The band were very professional, and some of the songs produced a genuinely psychotic atmosphere, but it was really a big anticlimax, and we realised that our perception of them was all wrong.'

The British underground continually aped bohemian America, and its non-recognition of reality made the British hippie movement seem even more esoteric than it already was. The Doors, unwittingly, had put a temporary halt to this American imperialism. When, during 'The End', Morrison repeated the line 'Father, I want to kill you', one indignant member of the audience shouted 'Bloody carnivore!'

In the dressing room after the show, Morrison was in a sullen mood, brushing off compliments, and pouring yet more booze down his throat. This caused some consternation among the hippy cognoscenti who had made it backstage. In those days alcohol had redneck connotations, and it didn't matter if you were the lead singer with the hippest band in America, drinking was still uncool. Morrison was oblivious, sodden, sinking more and more into his shell. This was his third persona of the day, and as luck would have it the easiest to adopt.

The hip might not have been entirely convinced by the Doors' European debut, but the hype surrounding their visit worked wonders, with 'Hello I Love You' becoming their most successful British hit (it reached number 15) and *Waiting for the Sun* eventually reaching number 16. The TV documentary *The Doors Are Open* received a positive critical response, and, despite coming across rather badly in a rambling, monotone interview, Morrison liked the film too, his only criticism being that it was rather obvious: 'The thing is, the guys that made the film had a thesis of what it was going to be before we came over. We were going to be the political rock group, and it also gave them the chance to whip out some of their anti-American sentiments, which they thought we were going to portray, and so they had their whole film before we came over.'

For Morrison, the rest of the European tour was a blur, a litany of alcohol and drug abuse, the singer spending most of his free time either drunk, or asleep, sometimes in a hotel bedroom, but other times sprawled out on the pavement. Give or take the odd debacle, the group's performances were usually up to scratch, though they were already performing on autopilot. Manzarek, Krieger and Densmore were merely going through the motions, while Morrison often had trouble remembering what those motions were. In the interviews he gave during this period, you can hear the timidity in his voice, as if he didn't really care whether or not he made himself understood.

Jefferson Airplane's lead singer Grace Slick remembers Morrison vividly. She said he reminded her of 'a rabid Johnny Depp, perfectly formed and possessed by abstraction'. She also remembers what she describes as his 'colourful non sequiturs', but which in print simply looks like Morrison's attempts to make himself appear more interesting.

"'Jim," I'd say, "did you see that broken chair by the speaker system?"

'With a pleasant smile and pupils dilated to the very edges of the iris, he'd respond with something like, "Lady in smoke shop, nobody for broken, chair broken, chair broken."'

Even though he was fond of talking gibberish, Slick seduced him on the tour. 'He was a well-built boy, his cock was slightly larger than average, and he was young enough to maintain the engorged silent connection right through the residue of chemicals that can threaten erection.'

Slick described their time in Holland: 'Both bands were walking down this street in Amsterdam, one of the main streets . . . and the kids would offer us drugs. We'd say, "Thanks very much," [and] put it in [our] pockets . . . but you wouldn't take everything you would be given otherwise you'd be dead.

'Jim, on the other hand, took everything that was given to him, on the spot.'

The European tour also introduced both groups to 'poppers' (amyl nitrate), and Morrison was such a fan of the drug that he used to come running on to the stage like a pinwheel. One night, when Jefferson Airplane were performing, he invaded the stage and started dancing along to one of their songs, blitzed out of his mind. He then collapsed, and was rushed to hospital in a portable oxygen tent. Later that night the Doors played as a three-piece, Ray Manzarek filling in for Morrison on vocals. It was not one of their most successful performances.

5

Aping the Changeling

By the end of 1968 the Doors were the most popular group in America, as well as the most controversial. Because they were so popular, their exploits were blown out of all proportion. Larger than life, and twice as ugly, the Doors represented the mood of the nation, the Zeitgeist incarnate. Morrison himself was still considered to be the sexiest man in rock and roll, in spite of the fact that he spent most of his time stupefied by alcohol and benzedrine, and in spite of being labeled the 'Mickey Mouse de Sade' by many of those who worked for him.

Danny Fields regularly felt the brunt of Morrison's sadistic personality: 'He really was a terror – he was the epitome of the old-fashioned concept of a brat, a big, brilliant, sexy brat. They don't make them like that any more, people who have that way of reacting to the world. These days pop stars are different when you try and talk to them about the realities of the business, or about what's required of them as a human being; they stop being bad boys. Morrison, he was an original. Of course it was all contrived – the macho pose thing – but he lived it, and underneath he didn't give a damn. Didn't give a damn about money, property, obsessions . . . he was one of the few people from that period who was genuinely anti-bourgeois. I suppose the hedonism got in the way.'

'His life, such as it was, was an open book,' said Steve Harris. 'This was the first time a pop performer had been so explicit in public, and he left nothing to the imagination. He lived his image to the hilt.'

The new tour got under way in November, the biggest the Doors had yet undertaken, and their fans reacted with an unexpected fervour. The group caused pandemonium almost everywhere they played, and there were riots in Phoenix, Cleveland, St Louis and Chicago. They had become satanic beat messiahs, a carnival freak-show, and the crowds came baying for blood, expecting some kind of unholy resurrection. Seeing the Doors was now a real experience, what with the unruly crowds, the band's increasingly sinister sound, and the performance of Morrison himself crawling around the stage dishevelled and drunk, sneering, swearing and hurling abuse at the audience. Unbeknown to the rest of the band, Morrison was deliberately courting violence at these concerts, manipulating the crowds into a frenzy.

'I was less theatrical, less artificial when I first began performing,' said Morrison of his stagecraft. 'But now the audiences are much larger and the rooms we play much bigger, it's necessary to project more – to exaggerate – almost to the point of grotesqueness.'

A big influence on Morrison at this point was a drama group called the Living Theatre – disciples of one of Morrison's heroes, the radical French dramatic theorist Antonin Artaud. Morrison had been infatuated with the group's activities for years, but now that the Doors' stage shows were becoming predictable and perfunctory, he began trying to incorporate the Living Theatre's ideas of confrontation and shock into his own performances.

If there is one event which led to Morrison's ultimate demise, it was the performance at the University of Southern California on 28 February 1969 by the Living Theatre. Here, Morrison saw the group enact their pièce de résistance, *Paradise Now*, an exercise in crowd manipulation. Including the repetition of several key phrases meant to drive the audience into a frenzy, *Paradise Now* was a guerrilla theatre performance, an aggressive spectacle, a serious art statement about censorship and freedom of speech. At the climax of the show the performers stripped off their clothes to the legal limit, though the police moved in and stopped the display before any of them got very far. Morrison was transfixed.

The next day the Doors were due to play Miami, their first ever concert in Florida. After a fight with Pamela which delayed him in LA, Morrison followed the rest of the band east, missing his connecting flights and drinking heavily. He arrived so late in Miami that the band went onstage an hour late. The rest of the band were already furious because the promoter had crammed far too many people into the auditorium, making the atmosphere hot and uncomfortable. The crowd themselves were hot and hungry: they were crushed together like animals, the band were late and the stories of earlier riots were passing around the auditorium like wildfire. Everyone felt the same: tonight was going to be special, tonight was going to be *real*.

Manzarek, Krieger and Densmore eventually crept onstage and began playing, hoping Morrison would join them. Eventually he did, but it was plain to all three of them that he was far drunker than he usually was when he fell onstage. The trip from Los Angeles had obviously taken its toll, as he could hardly stand up. The band ploughed through the material, making it more than obvious when they expected Morrison to come in with a vocal, but the singer was more interested in swearing at the audience, and muttering obscenities to himself. He'd start joining in with the band, then stop after a verse and a half to berate the audience some more. Here was the vulgar poet in all his drunk and disorderly glory, wrapping himself around the mike stand, belching, grabbing his crotch, gobbling the microphone like it was a rapidly melting ice cream.

'Anybody here from Tallahassee?' he enquired. After an affirmative response he hit back with, 'Well, I lived there once. I lived there until I got smart and went to California.'

From there it was downhill all the way: 'You're all a bunch of fucking idiots, how much longer are you going to let them push you around? You love it, you're all a bunch of slaves, what are you going to do about it? I'm not talking about getting out on the streets, I'm talking about having some fun, I'm talking about dancing, I'm talking about love your neighbour, till it hurts, I'm talking about grab your friend, I'm talking about love, love, love, love. Hey! Listen, I'm lonely, I need some love, y'all. Ain't nobody gonna love my ass? Come on, I need you. There's so many of you out there, ain't nobody gonna love me? Sweetheart, come on. Hey! How about fifty or sixty of you people come up here and love my ass? Come on!'

And with that, Morrison began taking off his clothes, throwing his shirt over his shoulder and unbuttoning his trousers. The drunken gibberish over with, he wanted to show the crowd what he was really made of.

The Living Theatre's Situationist striptease was being acted out by a paralytic pop star in front of thousands of screaming fans in a concert hall in Miami. Morrison imagined himself under the Klieg lights now, giving the finger to the world.

There are wildly conflicting reports about the subsequent exposure, and there have never been any photographs which show Morrison with his penis out. Yet he is supposed to have opened his leather trousers, displayed his partially erect penis and feigned masturbation. If true, it was hardly out of character.

Underwear and empty bottles were thrown at him during the striptease, but the debacle was cut short by a security guard who eventually pushed Morrison offstage. The concert had lasted just forty-five minutes.

Though this was the most explosive concert the band had so far performed, the press took a while to respond. But within a few days it was evident that Morrison had not got away with it. When the news of Morrison's exposure was substantiated, the police department and the state attorney's office came down heavily on the band, and Morrison was charged with everything from lewd and lascivious behaviour to indecent exposure, drunkenness and profanity. This sent terror through the Doors camp: if found guilty he could be sent down for seven years, effectively ending their career.

The press went crazy: exaggerated reports of the concert appeared all over the country, and the Doors became the *bête noire* of American rock and roll. The *Miami Herald* wrote: 'Included in the audience were hundreds of unescorted junior and senior high girls . . . It was not meant to be pretty. Morrison appeared to masturbate in full view of his audience, screamed obscenities, and exposed himself. He also got violent, shrugged off several officials and threw one of them off the stage before he himself was hurled into the crowd.'

In Florida a decency rally was organised, and across the nation all manner of public servants came out of the woodwork, denouncing Morrison as the devil himself. In a fit of moral panic, even the FBI got in on the act, issuing a warrant for Morrison's arrest and charging him with 'unlawful flight', even though he had left Miami three days before the warrants were issued. Before the concert Morrison had worried that the band were becoming public property; now they were public enemies – and he was Public Enemy Number One.

In Miami Morrison purposely tried to start a riot, but only succeeded in drawing attention to himself. Like many performers, he was unable to harness his own stardom, and because of this, began lampooning himself. Morrison couldn't cope with being a star because he didn't believe in what his fans believed in: himself. So he took it out on the rest of the group, then the audience, and then himself. He was dismissive of his audience because he held them in contempt. They treated him like a god, yet he knew he was only a puppet of the crowd; they weren't interested in his literary allegories, they wanted him to make a spectacle of himself. Morrison had now failed on two counts. First, he had been unsuccessful in killing off his creation. Secondly, the whole affair was an embarrassment: he was being persecuted for *perhaps* exposing himself. In Britain a few years previously, P. J. Proby's career had been cut short by a succession of trouser-splitting performances, but in America Morrison's performance in Miami was the first time since Elvis that indecent exposure by a pop star had caused so much controversy. It would become commonplace, with many rock stars exposing their private parts for public consumption, but in 1969 it was heresy.

As a sign of defeat, after Miami Morrison put away the leather trousers, swapping them for black jeans and baggy cotton pants. Because of his stomach, his shirts changed too, and he took to wearing white muslin Mexican shirts which he let hang down outside his belt. He also let his beard grow, and his hair began to turn grey.

The band needed to tour, but found this almost impossible – they immediately lost thirty concerts because of Miami. At the few concerts they managed to organise they had to put up a $5,000 bond – a 'fuck clause', as they called it – in case Morrison disgraced himself. And the audiences came expecting the very same, and were disappointed when he let them down. His trousers safely zipped up, Morrison roamed the stage, hamming it up, contemptuously singing 'Light My Fire' while sneering at the audience. But if he appeared angry, inside he was sad. Interviewed for *Rolling Stone* by Jerry Hopkins soon after Miami, Morrison showed a new maturity and even voiced a few regrets. He was tired and frustrated, wounded and scared. Was a new Jim Morrison emerging? More contemplative, and extremely paranoid, the new Jim Morrison suddenly looked like the unhappiest rock star in the world.

In one of his last interviews, with Bob Chorush of the *Los Angeles Free Press* in 1971, Morrison said, 'The Doors never really had any riots. I did try and create something a few times just because I'd always heard about riots at concerts, and I thought we ought to have [one]. So I tried to stimulate a few little riots, and after a few times I realised it's such a joke. It doesn't lead anywhere. You know what, soon it got to the point where people didn't think it was a successful concert unless everybody jumped up and ran around a bit.'

While in London Morrison had met the poet Michael McClure, who was extremely excited by the singer's poetry, and urged him to get it published. Back in Los Angeles, with time on his hands, Morrison set to work, determined to make his poetry public. But McClure was one of the few who had faith in Morrison's poems: 'I was always disappointed that the poetry didn't measure up to the songs,' said Patricia Kennealy, the girl Morrison would soon marry. 'They weren't much. I think he would have possibly gotten better at it as he went along, but I found the ones he did write very self-indulgent and self-referential. But he was young.' While the Doors were on hold, Morrison threw himself into his poetry, eventually persuading Simon and Schuster to publish two volumes.

During February 1969 a new Doors single 'Touch Me' climbed to number three in the American charts, becoming a million seller. The band must have thought themselves lucky, as the song was not only their weakest single so far, but it also featured plenty of brass as well as a string ensemble. Fans were shocked, though not quite enough to ignore the record. But the worst was yet to come. If *Waiting for the Sun* had been a disappointment, then *The Soft Parade*, the Doors' fourth album, was little short of a tragedy. Originally planned as the band's *Sgt. Pepper*, it turned out to be the worst record they ever made, taking over a year to record and costing nearly $100,000. For the first time the songs bore individual writing credits, with Robby Krieger responsible for over half the album and most of the lacklustre compositions.

Because Morrison had not written many songs – he was concentrating on his poetry – he wanted to distance himself from those of Krieger, and insisted on the individual credits.

Everything on *The Soft Parade* was well below par: 'Wishful Sinful', another single from the LP, only reached number 44, while 'Tell All the People' and its follow-up, 'Runnin' Blue', did even worse. All were written by Krieger.

Morrison washed his hands of the affair, and as he didn't really care about the music any more it was no surprise when the group started to deteriorate. Morrison was experiencing his own decline and fall and, suffering the onslaught of the press, retreated into himself.

The Soft Parade is still viewed as the Doors' nadir: 'Tell All the People' is a ridiculous Pied Piper overture, the kind of paint-by-number ditty that could have been produced by any number of bands. 'Touch Me' is an unsuccessful rerun of 'Light My Fire' (throughout their career the group would continue to rework the 'Light My Fire' formula, with songs like 'Touch Me', 'Hello I Love You' and 'Love Me Two Times'); while 'Runnin' Blue' is simply bizarre. This song, a tribute to the recently deceased Otis Redding, features completely inappropriate bluegrass fiddles and mandolins.

Interviews from the time, in which he would ramble more than usual, reflected Morrison's general malaise: 'It used to seem possible to generate a move-ment – people rising up and joining together in a mass protest – refusing to be represented any longer – like, they'd all put their strength together to break what Blake calls "the mind-forged manacles" ... The Love Street times are dead. Sure, it's possible for there to be a transcendence – but not on a mass level, not a univer-sal rebellion. Now it has to take place on an individual level – every man for himself, as they say. Save yourself. Violence isn't always evil. What's evil is the infatuation with violence.'

Except for a few rare occasions, Morrison didn't come across well in interviews. While he was certainly outgoing, and talked a lot about his work, in print he always seemed to be reciting lines. He gave good copy, but never appeared to give much of himself, even when explaining some deep and obviously personal philosophical point. He would talk for hours about shamanism, or his role as an idol, and then deflate it with a sarcastic and often self-deprecating remark. When journalists saw that he could turn his soul-searching monologues on and off like a light switch, it made them wary. Even the writers who went on bar crawls with him, who spent days in his company, never felt much warmth. They couldn't crack the code.

Morrison fell back on abstractions: 'I'm not sure it's salvation that people are after, or want me to lead them to. The shaman is a healer like the witch-doctor. I don't see people turning to me for that. I don't see myself as a savior. The shaman is similar to the scapegoat. I see the role of the artist as shaman and scapegoat. People project their fantasies onto him and their fantasies come alive. People can destroy their fantasies by destroying him. I obey the impulses everyone has, but won't admit to. By attacking me, punishing me, they can feel relieved of those impulses.'

Self-aggrandising, self-absorbed, self-obsessed? Completely.

The drink, the drugs and the endless supply of women were the consolation prize for knowing he could never really win. Being a star meant he had several career options open to him: he could burn out, throw away his credibility and let his fans crucify him, or he could die. Either way, Morrison knew it couldn't last. So while the Doors released mediocre records, Morrison continued his extracurricular activities, organising the publication of *The Lords* and *The New Creatures*, and starting work on a new movie. After forming his own production company, Morrison hired a few friends and asked them to interpret an amorphous idea he had for a film. *Hwy*, as it was eventually called, was almost a sequel to the first film he'd made back in college. It included the usual Morrison symbolism: hitchhikers in the desert, peyote and coyotes, and death on the road. Early footage also featured the daredevil rock star walking along an eighteen-inch-wide ledge on top of a seventeen-storey building on Sunset Boulevard. When the crew expressed alarm at this proposal, Morrison – typically drunk, typically stubborn – danced along the ledge without his safety rope, urinating as he went.

The band suffered a terrible backlash from the press. On the one hand they were savaged by the music critics for making such a misguided record; on the other they were hounded by the national press for their contribution to the decline of American moral values.

But though the critics were merciless, some understood why Morrison was going off the rails. Liza Williams, writing in the *Los Angeles Free Press* in early 1969, was more than aware that Morrison had become public property: 'He is the ultimate Barbie doll, and Barbie speaks when we pull her string, that's what she's supposed to do, and she only says what we want her to say because you see on the other end of the string is a piece of tape, that's why she is our Barbie doll and that's why he is our Jim Morrison and that's why we want him to sing 'Light My Fire' and stop Stop STOP all these other strange sentences that the doll didn't say when we bought her, these new words on the tape, she has no right to new words, just do her thing.'

This was no consolation for Morrison, who had never wanted his teenybopper audience, always striving for 'adult' acclaim. 'The band were always popular with the little girls and with the older, more serious rock fans,' said Danny Fields. 'But when he lost his original, extremely hip, older college audience, it was the little girls who kept him in the charts. It was the little girls who made "Touch Me" a smash, the little girls who put *The Soft Parade* into the charts, the little girls who made him rich.'

Even before the disaster in Miami, things were looking decidedly grim for the Doors. At the 18,000-seater Forum in Los Angeles in January 1969, the strain was beginning to show. The audience were not so enthusiastic about the new material from *The Soft Parade*, and kept asking for songs from the first album. The band members were also spending less and less time together. Manzarek, Krieger and Densmore were very protective about their image and the myth surrounding the group, but Morrison was finding it increasingly difficult to communicate with them, and after a while began to think of the Doors simply as his backing band. After Miami, Morrison had purposely taken stock of himself; he had become quieter and more reflective, preferring his own company.

But while he internalised his emotions, his body went to seed: the small paunch was soon not so small and his beard hung down over his chest. He was noticeably shaken and there were worrying signs of wear and tear.

Danny Fields recalled that 'his looks had gone by this point. When his cheeks puffed up from the alcohol his eyes disappeared and he got this sort of pig face. His beauty was gone. He knew his days as an idol were over. Jim Morrison was like Dorian Gray in reverse – he was visibly deteriorating in front of his public. But they always expected him to be as beautiful as he used to be. Nevertheless, he seemed to have acquired some wisdom, balance, a sense of humour ... a sort of warmth. He had a sense of self-understanding, and a humility that I had thought he was incapable of. It took losing that fiery look for him to become a human being.'

Humility was a trait which didn't sit well with Morrison, and as soon as the shock of the Miami episode wore off he resumed his self-destruction.

The days were no longer bright, but they were still filled with pain. When he awoke, sick, hungover, with another strange girl straddling his paunch, he could always vindicate himself by slowly repeating William Blake's sagacious words of calm: 'The road of excess leads to the palace of Wisdom.' He may have had a gift for writing songs about his emotions, but common sense appeared to elude him.

As Liza Williams has observed, Morrison allowed himself to become a mirror for the ghoulish adoration of his fans, and after a while he became their fantasy. He became a screen onto which the audience projected their own fantasies. But if Morrison's life was just one long movie, it was ultimately a snuff movie, starring himself. 'With people,' recalled Patricia Kennealy, 'he was whatever they expected him to be. Some people said he was almost like a mirror, just reflecting whatever you were. If you were expecting him to be the Prince of Darkness, he would oblige you. I told him once that I thought he was the shyest person that I'd ever met and that he had to create a sensation as a sort of cover-up. He thought that was just incredibly perceptive and very mean of me to say so.'

Kennealy is convinced that the Jim Morrison she knew was the one and only Morrison, but there are countless people with whom he collided who think they knew him too.

'In almost every case, even his most casual acquaintances firmly believe that they alone were privileged to see "the real Jim",' said Mick Farren. 'They all claim that Morrison subjected everyone else but them to the games and experiments. Only with them did he shed the Lizard King armour. We have no way of telling if Morrison, in fact, ever dropped the role. The only thing that's certain is that he took a spoiled child's delight in feeding the fantasies of everyone he met. In so doing he may have lost a great deal of his own personality.'

By the summer of 1969 it was painfully clear to everyone who knew him that Morrison was falling apart, lost in his own weird orbit of fame. His drinking was taking over his life, his pretty-boy looks had gone and he was getting terribly fat: hardly an icon of the new age, he was an overweight soak. His face was puffy, his hair matted and dank. He hardly ever washed, and wore the same trousers for weeks on end. When the Doors realised his vanity had deserted him, it made them worry because they knew he didn't care any more. And that meant obsolescence. His life was one long bar crawl, beginning when he awoke and ending when he fell over, some fourteen hours later, somewhere in Hollywood, with a beer bottle in one hand and a blonde in the other (when asking for a blow job he'd say, 'Suck my mama').

Judging from a 1969 interview he gave to the legendary *Village Voice* writer and documentary maker Howard Smith, Morrison was always fairly ambivalent about his size, and while he obviously enjoyed the attention his body drew from his legions of fans, his descent into obesity seems almost deliberate.

'Why is it so onerous to be fat?' he asked Smith, rhetorically. 'I remember when I used to weigh 185 pounds. I was the same height that I now am. I was going to college, and I had this food ticket at the cafeteria. And the food is mainly all based on starch – cheap food, right? And so I don't know what it was – I just felt like if I missed a meal, I was getting screwed, right? So I'd get up at 6:30 every morning just to make breakfast. Eggs and grits and sausages and toast. Milk. Then I'd go do a few classes and I'd make it in there for lunch. Mashed potatoes, ahh. Every now and then, they'd put a little piece of meat in something, you know? And then I'd go to a few more classes and then I'd go to dinner and it was more mashed potatoes.

'So about three months later, I was 185 pounds, and you know what? I felt so great. I felt like a tank, you know? I felt like a large mammal, a big beast. When I'd move through the corridors or across the lawn, I just feel like I could knock anybody out of my way. I was solid, man. It's terrible to be thin and wispy because, you know, you'd get knocked over by a strong wind or something. Fat is beautiful.'

His performances were no longer cathartic, only a slow form of public suicide. During concerts he would mercilessly taunt the squirming girls in the front rows with screams and torrents of abuse, often spitting at his astonished pupils. His sweat-blurred eyes would burn holes in their faces as he lashed them with his tongue. He'd stalk the stage with an erection plainly visible through his trousers, daring anyone to touch. Backstage he would flick lighted cigarettes at groupies and demand oral sex, regardless of who was watching.

Morrison wasn't a diabolist, and neither was he an adorable monster. Rather he was a fantasist, so convinced of his own talent that he became dismissive of everyone around him. Neither was he especially predatory, and would usually wait for women to approach him. He wasn't particularly choosy, and would often slip away from a party with women who wouldn't normally be considered to be in his league. Morrison would sit in the band's dressing room before or after concerts, allowing any groupie who had managed to get backstage to kneel in front of him and fellate him, regardless of whether anyone was in the room. He'd just sit there, swigging from whatever bottle happened to be in his hand, as a girl worked away between his legs. His drinking bouts were now so extreme, and his drug intake so huge, that the band were in constant fear for his life. He had turned into a perpetual drunk: abusive and violent, melancholic and tearful. Hustling around the mid-rise scatter of Hollywood, he'd vomit in hallways, out of car windows, in people's apartments, at recording sessions, in bed, on the lavatory, in the bath – Morrison was sick everywhere.

One particularly brattish trick was urinating in public: at a film awards ceremony in Atlanta he emptied his bursting bladder into an empty wine bottle and put it back on the table where it was eventually drunk. Once, at Max's in LA, he pissed in a wine bottle and presented it to the waitress, asking her to take it home as he couldn't finish it himself. One night in New York, in a small club off Columbus Circle near Central Park, drinking Mexican beer with Steve Harris, he turned to the Elektra Vice President and said: 'You know the difference between me and you? The difference is that I could throw this bottle against that mirror, smash it, and in the morning I wouldn't have any guilt. None.'

'He was an alcoholic, plain and simple,' said Harris. 'It wasn't because of the pressure – if times were good he drank, if times were bad he drank. If the sun was shining he drank, if it was raining he drank. It was as simple as that. And yes, he was obnoxious. Some people are sweet drunks, but Jim was a redneck – gross, obnoxious and rude. You couldn't tell him anything; he was a complete sociopath.'

With the band unable to tour, Morrison was free to indulge himself as much as he liked. Pamela Courson was at this point also allowing him an unusual amount of freedom. Ever since the Doors had become stars she had found herself unable to deal with the attention Morrison received – she disliked most of his friends, and was constantly on the lookout for girls trying to worm their way into Jim's affections. Nor could she cope with his increasingly debauched lifestyle, and to compensate had begun dating a number of men. It got to the stage where she would go out with the specific intention of being picked up, solely to annoy him. She felt unfulfilled, and by this time was already using heroin, though she hadn't told Jim yet. He tried to placate her with endless expensive presents, by letting her go shopping in his chauffeured limousine, and even bought her a clothes boutique which she tried to run, but she still couldn't cope. There were constant furious fights between them, after which they usually drove off in separate directions looking for someone to spend the night with. Recently, though, the fights had been getting worse, and while Courson would wander the bars of the Strip loaded on depressants and heroin, Morrison would trawl the other side of town, looking for his own action. So, instead of staying in with Courson, or going to the many record company meetings, photo sessions and recording sessions, Morrison would spend his days cruising bars and joyriding in the hills outside LA, or dreaming up obscure film projects for himself and his friends. (Morrison now saw film as the only way he could truly express himself, and devoted much of his time to the *Hwy* movie, wary of the Hollywood producers who, he thought, 'just want to hang my meat on the screen'.) He would drop in to see his new friend Alice Cooper rehearse, often dragging one of Cooper's band out to his car and forcing him to race up to the Hollywood Hills. Once there, Morrison would demand whoever was driving to go as fast as possible while he threw himself out. This was how he liked to top off an evening, by getting involved in some foolish daredevil scheme which would invariably lead to a drunken act of bravery. He drank to build up enough courage to do something stupid, whether it was throwing himself out of a speeding car or picking a fight with someone twice his size. He constantly tried to prove himself, and yet wasn't too upset if he got beaten up. Winning wasn't important, it was taking part, taking the risk. 'He was always on the edge of reality,' said Krieger, although he made it sound like a compliment.

Now that Morrison was relinquishing any interest he might have in the real world, Elektra found him impossible to work with. 'He was such an asshole,' said Danny Fields. 'But was that his problem, or mine? At the time I wished it had only been his problem. But when you're working for someone, and when they're paying the bills, it becomes your problem.'

'Of course, there were worries about the way he conducted himself,' said Steve Harris, 'because at that time FM rock radio had not really come into its own, and the AM stations liked everything and everybody to be hunky dory. After the New Haven bust, all the stations stopped playing "Love Me Two Times", which was out at the time. But as the LP kept selling, after a while people accepted him for what he was. So we went along with it, we left him alone.'

What Morrison had more than anything was self-belief. He had it deep inside him, real as an organ. Today the world is awash with those who expect to be able to inflict their egos and personality on anyone with a mobile phone or a laptop – be it through a self-published art book, a personalised T-shirt, a bespoke mountain bike, a tweet, a Facebook post or a Pinterest board – although when Morrison first started stumbling around LA, the cult of personality had yet to be commodified. He had what Orson Welles had always been accused of: 'excessive showmanship'.

He was the hipster personified, in literary critic Anatole Broyard's words, keeping tabs 'like a suspicious proprietor, on his environment. He stood always a little apart from the group. His feet solidly planted, his shoulders drawn up, his elbows in, hands pressed to sides, he was a pylon around whose implacability the world obsequiously careered.'

With the world falling about his ears, Morrison sought refuge in the arms of Patricia Kennealy, one of the shrewdest things he ever did. Meeting Patricia Kennealy was the best thing that could have happened to him at this time, and she was probably the most important influence on him during his last years. They came together like colliding trains.

The couple had first met earlier in the year when Kennealy had interviewed him for the East Coast rock magazine *Jazz & Pop*, where she was Editor-in-Chief. She had written extensively on the band before their meeting, and continued to afterwards. But while she was a fan, she was no sycophant, attacking Morrison in print for his verbosity and grandiose mannerisms long before she did it to his face.

Kennealy was extremely attractive, but she had two other qualities which drew Morrison to her: she was his intellectual equal, and she wouldn't take any bullshit – if she thought he was stringing her a line, she told him so.

Kennealy developed something of a reputation with the band and Morrison's record company, and she had a reputation for being a practising white witch, so for years after Morrison's death no one would go near her. As no one had ever interviewed her before – they appeared to be too scared – I began looking for her in New York. I spoke with Elektra Records, and with the thirty or so people I interviewed for this book, in London, New York and Los Angeles, but not only could none of them point me in the right direction, some advised me to steer clear of her completely. 'She's dangerous,' I was told. 'She'll eat you alive.' In the end it took me about forty minutes to track her down, simply by looking through the New York phone directory. And she was charm personified.

'I was knocked out by his manners the first time I met him,' she said. 'He stood up and shook my hand as I walked into the hotel room for the interview, and a rock star had never done that before. I was obviously overawed because he was already a hero of mine, but I was staggered by how literate he was. I thought rock stars were mostly jerks before I met Jim. Music meant a lot at that point, and it was annoying to discover that the people making it were mostly dumb. Jim definitely had a brain. His songs were sometimes too contrived, but they had a certain quality that was different to everything else. He was funny too: I mentioned to him that at one of his concerts two spotlights had come together on him and formed a cross. He snapped back, quick as a flash with, "A cross is the cheapest thing to do, man, all you need is two sticks."

'He was much funnier when he was sober, but then I guess most of us are. Mostly when he was drunk with me he would get kind of quiet and surly. But he was never at a loss for words.'

It took a while for them to become lovers – theirs was an old-fashioned courtship – but when they finally did, like Morrison and Pamela Courson they became inseparable. 'It was a very personal thing, and the fact that he was famous didn't seem to intrude upon it at all. I suppose that indicates a kind of ostrich mentality on my part, thinking we could walk around Central Park without anyone noticing. But for me it was as though we existed inside a bubble. Of course it wasn't true.'

The bubble burst when Kennealy saw how he could behave in front of other people. 'He gave people what perhaps he seemed to think they expected of him. He was rather obliging in respect of his drinking. I don't think the person I met was an act, I thought the Jim Morrison I knew was the real person. I might have been naive as hell, but I thought that this was what he was really like, and the other stuff – the drinking and the drugs – was extraneous. I thought he was a genuinely shy person, and the other stuff was a mask, a convenient persona for people to relate to. It was self-defence. But this side of his character manifested itself in a totally outrageous and malevolent way, and it became larger than he was. His success magnified his human weaknesses.'

Kennealy tried to pull Morrison back to earth, but as soon as she'd persuaded him to stop drinking, split from the band and concentrate on living his life, he'd recoil and turn back into the Pigman from LA.

'At the time I thought, if this is as good as it can get, then this is what I'll have to settle for. I would rather have had what I had, than not have had anything. He would always say that it was over between him and Pamela, that the relationship was half pity, but he never would have left her.'

At this stage, Kennealy was one of the few people trying to get Morrison to slow down. To others he was simply a wild rock and roller. 'In those days,' said Steve Harris, 'people didn't think in terms of cleaning up their acts – record companies didn't ask bands to lay off the booze for a while because an important gig was coming up. There was none of that, basically because there wasn't the knowledge that there is now. That was the first period when people went for it in a serious way. Now, years later, those people are either dead, they've cleaned up, or they're vegetables. The records were still selling, so why should we have tried to stop him? We thought: so, he drinks, everybody drinks, right? Rehabilitation would never have worked because he just didn't want it.'

'I tried to stop him, but by then he was too far gone,' said Kennealy. 'It had got so out of hand I don't think he could have gone off and been the semi-private person he would have liked to have been. He was beginning to fall apart, on all levels, just sliding downhill. I felt useless; I would have sold my soul to stop it. It was just so inevitable; it was like a Greek tragedy after a while. It just got worse, and worse and worse. No one could do a damn thing about it. We'd talk, argue, scream, and nothing would change. It didn't seem to be anything he could do anything about.

'He was too entrenched in all the bullshit. I would tell him he was surrounded by assholes, and he would laugh and say, yes, he knew. What can you do? You can't kidnap someone and deprogram them. Maybe you can, but it wasn't something that would have occurred to me at the time. People can't be saved unless they want to be saved, and Jim didn't. I think he had this idea that once he was saved he wouldn't be an artist any more. It was this whole romantic Hemingway thing.

'He thought he could become a serious artist by being a rock singer, but just found the whole thing relentlessly trivialised by his fans. It depressed him when he realised that people only saw him as a rock star, and that he probably didn't control his own life or destiny any more. It was really sad – he should have cut out a hell of a lot sooner.'

By the end of 1969 Jim Morrison was a sex symbol with a paunch and a beard. He was fat, drunk and unhappy. Strapped to a rollercoaster which showed no signs of slowing down, he was rushing through life with no sense of purpose, all his sensibilities blurred by drink. As all around him the pressure and tension built up, he became a frenzied zombie, a walking corpse, a man who only wanted escape.

This was hardly surprising, as Morrison's life had recently become a litany of disasters: during November he had entered a 'not guilty' plea to charges as a result of the incident in Miami, and had been released on $5,000 bail.

Two days later he was arrested after flying to Phoenix with Tom Baker and a few drinking buddies, ostensibly to see the Rolling Stones; he was charged with being drunk and disorderly and interfering with the flight of an aircraft, after being rowdy and apparently molesting an air stewardess. The charges were eventually dropped.

The documentary film *Feast of Friends* was finally released, and was described by *Variety* as a failure, 'made either from the out-takes of some larger project or an unsold try at daytime-TV slotted to meet the kids home from school'. *Rolling Stone*, meanwhile, simply called it pretentious, although the film won an award at the Atlanta Film Festival. And *Hwy*, another film close to his heart, was screened to a resolutely unenthusiastic reception. He was courted to appear in several movies – including one marshalled by Steve McQueen – but nothing came of them.

To console himself, Morrison continued on his drinking binges, but increasingly he was unaccompanied. (Tom Baker, perhaps his closest drinking buddy, had fallen out with Morrison after the Phoenix trip.) His twenty-sixth birthday was celebrated at Bill Siddons' house in Manhattan Beach, where Morrison repaid his hospitality by falling asleep on the couch, his penis poking out of his trousers and soaking the carpet with piss. Because he was turning into such a behemoth, and because the paranoia surrounding the band's performances had led to the cancellation of so many concerts, the rest of the band kept asking him to get his act together, to shave and shed a few pounds for their forthcoming dates in LA; but Morrison just ignored them. Miami had really taken its toll, and constant paternity suits only made him more insecure. Morrison began to look vulnerable. It was now that he first began mentioning a move to Paris as a possible means of escape. Elektra tried to combat the steadily increasing flow of bad publicity by relaunching Morrison as a Renaissance man, and various press releases outlining Morrison's genius were drawn up for his approval. Predictably, the singer wanted nothing to do with it: he didn't want the people told that he was a superman; he wanted them to discover it for themselves. One thing that did please Morrison was the publication of *The Lords* and *The New Creatures* in one volume by Simon and Schuster, even though it was credited to Jim Morrison, and not James Douglas Morrison, as he'd requested.

In February 1970 the group released their fifth LP, *Morrison Hotel* (named after a real $2 skid-row hotel in downtown LA). After the disappointment of *The Soft Parade*, this was almost a return to form, though by no means a complete success. The record contained some strong, evocative songs. 'Peace Frog' made reference to the horrific car accident Morrison had witnessed as a child, where he claimed the souls of various American Indians entered his 'fragile eggshell mind'. 'Queen of the Highway' was inspired by Courson. 'Roadhouse Blues', with its flagrantly ironic blues lyric – Morrison guzzling beer as soon as he wakes up – was the story of Morrison's life. But somehow everyone expected more. It was as if the Doors had lost their social context.

Rock critic Robert Christgau's reaction to the album was typical: 'As he [Morrison] discovers his real affection for rock and roll music . . . he uncovers his inability to relate wholeheartedly to it. Suddenly, Morrison's timbre loses much of its former mystery, his phrasing lacks wit, and the music, while competent enough, excites only those over on the persona he once managed to project with such ferocious intensity – those entranced by an afterimage, so to speak.

'For although Morrison once made music that was good as music, music was never his specialty, and consequently it was never the strength of the group he defined. The Doors were film students, remember, and their deepest passion was communication, which Morrison called "politics". Only Robby Krieger was a musician by commitment, and, given a few bad breaks, the group might very well have disbanded as quickly as it succeeded. When their success became perfunctory, so did their music.'

Ever counter-intuitive, Hunter S. Thompson loved it: 'Crank it all the way up on one of those huge obsolete wire-burning MacIntosh amps and eighty custom-built speakers. Then stand back somewhere on the main beams of a big log house and feel the music come up through your femurs . . . and after that you can always say, for sure, that you once knew what it was like to hear men play rock and roll music.'

But if the music had become more pragmatic, a note of bitterness had crept into Morrison's interviews. He told *Creem* magazine at the time, 'The music has gotten progressively better, tighter, more professional, more interesting, but I think that people resent the fact that three years ago there was a great renaissance of spirit and emotion and revolutionary sentiment, and when things didn't change overnight I think people resented the fact that we were just still around doing good music.'

Two months after its release, *Morrison Hotel* was awarded a gold disc, making the Doors the first American rock group to achieve five gold albums in a row.

During the spring Morrison renewed his acquaintance with Patricia Kennealy. They had not had much contact since their first meetings eighteen months earlier, only exchanging the occasional letter, phone call or gift, but it was Kennealy whom Jim called when he doubted himself and needed to be told he was a god or a schmuck; and Kennealy who would tell him in no uncertain terms. His relationship with Courson might have been more habitual, but it was Kennealy who offered the intellectual firepower, who challenged him. When Jim showed Courson the lyrics to a new song, she'd tell him how marvellous he was; when he showed Kennealy, she'd point out its pretentious literary references. He was as abusive to her as he was to Courson, but Kennealy saw sides of him that no one else did. 'I saw him be a terrible pig,' she said. 'He was a pig to me and he was a pig to Pam, but I have the other stuff to balance against that. I was honest with him. Apart from me I don't think anyone was honest with him at that point. And because he couldn't trust anyone, he covered up. He had this really vulnerable psyche, this inner self that he genuinely wanted to protect, the way we all do. He threw up screens to protect himself, and sometimes he was successful, sometimes not.'

On Midsummer's Night 1970, at 10.30 p.m., after spending the day together, Morrison and Kennealy were married in her Gothic East Village apartment in New York. But this was no ordinary service; it was a Wicca wedding, a ceremony based on 'white' witchcraft. At this period in her life Kennealy was a practising member of a New York coven, and the ceremony was conducted by its founders, a high priest and priestess.

'What I practise is witchcraft, for want of a better word,' she said. 'It's esoteric Christianity. I've fallen out of the habit of covens and all that kind of stuff, but I would characterise myself more as a Pagan than a Christian. When I pray, it's not always to Jesus. I told Jim the first time I met him that I was involved in witchcraft – I was either so anaesthetised by drink or so incredibly comfortable that it just came out. He was surprised, sort of how you might be surprised if your cat suddenly started talking: you might be a bit intimidated, but on the whole, you'd rather like it.

'I suppose he felt a need for some kind of avowal of his feelings, a formalised connection, however unorthodox it might have been. The drama of the ceremony certainly appealed to him. It was an extraordinary experience, it was magical.'

Morrison and Kennealy took part in the ritual handfasting, and drew each other's blood, as part of the Celtic tradition. They mixed a few drops of their blood with consecrated wine, which they then drank, and then signed the official documents, one written in English, the other in runes. They then signed their names in blood, after which Morrison fainted.

'He fainted because he came into the presence of the Goddess, one of the ancient forces of nature, and one of the people to whom we pray,' Kennealy said. 'Being in a magical circle takes an awful lot out of you – it's very intense. It's an actual physical thing, and if you're not prepared for it – which Jim obviously wasn't – it's very powerful. Magic is a very real thing ... it's a draining of energy.'

Life sped on. There was no time to think, only drink . . . obliteration was the key. Soon after his bizarre marriage to Kennealy, Morrison visited Paris, scouring the city for apartments as well as visiting the bars. A week later he was back in LA, where he continued his excessive behaviour, one week being arrested for public drunkenness, the next catching pneumonia.

At a time when live performances by the group were sporadic, in July Elektra decided to release the Doors' first live album, a two-record package called *Absolutely Live*, which had been recorded in New York during January. It contained some good performances, but was only noteworthy for the inclusion of a full-blown version of 'Celebration of the Lizard'. The cover was a dead giveaway, featuring a photograph of Morrison which was at least eighteen months old; there was little point using a recent picture of the singer: he was too wan and fat.

The Miami trial began in August and was a farce from the outset. The prosecution paraded a seemingly endless procession of witnesses claiming to have seen Morrison expose himself, even though 150 photographs taken at the concert contradicted this. Miami versus Morrison was a sham – maybe because the odds were stacked against him from the start. His attorneys tried to sidestep the issue by comparing his stagecraft with other forms of contemporary 'art': things like the novel *Portnoy's Complaint*, the stage show *Hair!* and the film *Woodstock*, which included nudity, swearing and purposeful exhibitionism. It was a cunning ploy, but the judge nevertheless threw the idea out of court, declaring that examples of 'community standards' would not be admitted for evidence.

'It was a complete sham,' recalled Patricia Kennealy, who was at the trial. 'He was a scapegoat, taking the heat for a lot of other people.'

Morrison's problems were compounded when, on 14 August, Kennealy called him from New York to tell him she was pregnant with his child. After inviting her down to Miami, he systematically avoided her and refused to have anything to do with the impending birth. After a while he relented and talked it through, though they couldn't agree to keep the child. In the end he offered to pay for an abortion, and promised to be with her when it happened.

'We talked about having the baby for quite a while,' said Kennealy, 'which is why it went as long as it did [twenty weeks]. I had to face up to the fact that he probably wouldn't be around much, and really neither of us wanted the child anyway. It was terrible timing all round. I only really wanted the child because it was Jim's, and as he wasn't crazy about it, well . . .'

In the middle of the trial the band flew to England to appear at the Isle of Wight festival, which – despite strong competition – turned out to be one of their most chaotic performances. Morrison had been up for thirty-six hours when he went onstage, and his drinking had affected him so much he could hardly stand. The band hated the experience, hated playing outdoors in front of thousands of people they couldn't see or hear, and Morrison hated it so much he claimed he would never appear onstage again. By now, the whole band were sick of performing. As Robby Krieger said, 'At that time we didn't think we'd ever go out on the road again. We were contented to stay in LA and cut records. We'd had it with the police, hall managers, narcs and the vice squad. They were always there – with tapes, cameras, microphones. They were ready for anything.'

In September, after more than a month, the trial was finally over, Morrison having been found guilty of indecent exposure and profanity, though he was acquitted on the charge of 'lewd and lascivious behaviour'. He was released on $50,000 bail. He said to reporters after leaving the courtroom: 'This trial and its outcome won't change my style, because I maintain that I did not do anything wrong.'

Things went from bad to worse: Jimi Hendrix and Janis Joplin had just died, and Morrison would sit in the bars along Sunset Strip saying, 'You're drinking with number three.' What if he *was* next? He'd sit alone by the jukebox and ponder the question. Paranoia was getting the better of him: ask him at the wrong end of the day and he'd say his life was no longer worth living because it had become a living nightmare. He'd alienated most of his friends, the arguments with Courson and Kennealy were getting more intense, and he could no longer talk to Manzarek, Krieger or Densmore.

In Miami in October he was officially sentenced to eight months' hard labour and a $500 fine. He appealed. In November Kennealy had the abortion in New York. Morrison was not present; there were no flowers; he didn't even call.

'Looking back I'm astonished at what I let myself be put through,' said Kennealy. 'But I'm older now. He was only about the third boyfriend I'd had in my whole life, and I didn't have a whole lot of experience. Obviously he made me happy or else I wouldn't have put up with it for as long as I did.'

6

Wasting the Dawn

It's late 1970, and the recording of *LA Woman*, the Doors' sixth studio album, is going badly. Morrison, as drunk as ever, is even more unreliable than usual, and the frustration of the rest of the band is reaching new heights. Paul Rothchild has already walked out, claiming to be bored by their new songs, not wanting to hang around and produce 'cocktail music'. Bruce Botnick, their regular engineer, has replaced him, recording the band live in their rehearsal studios on Santa Monica Boulevard, right across the street from Elektra Records. To the band the songs sound good, though it's difficult getting Morrison into the studio to record them. Recording starts around one o'clock on most afternoons, with the singer turning up around five or six, completely drunk, having dragged himself from the Tropicana, the Chateau Marmont, the Alta Cienega or some other misery motel. When Morrison does eventually turn up, Botnick tries to record his vocals in one take, just in case he disappears again.

But Morrison's final offering wasn't as bad as Paul Rothchild originally thought. In fact, *LA Woman* is one of the most memorable Doors records, containing real red-letter music. The urgency has gone, and at times the record sounds contemplative and weary, but overall the feeling is one of menace and unease. On *LA Woman* Morrison managed to transform himself into an old blues singer, and for him, these dark, brooding songs seemed a dignified departure from the adolescent pop of their previous records. In his own mind, Morrison had something of a death wish now, and in hindsight, the record seems like a melancholy farewell. His voice, ravaged by drink and three packets of cigarettes a day, rode roughshod over the chromatic soundtrack, a brooding, menacing voice that even to the most casual listener sounded resigned, desperate, tired. He was a man exposed, a man saying goodbye in the only way he knew.

In many ways *LA Woman* exists on a bass line, a fat, linear throb: the title track is a road song, but as Los Angeles is only really a collection of roads, this makes perfect sense. Here Morrison depicts the anonymous, depraved urban jungle – not, as in 'People Are Strange', with wide-eyed wonder, but with regret. Morrison is bruised, and he wants to let us know. LA was a town of temptation for Morrison, but when he sings 'LA Woman', cataloguing the city's various highs and lows, it's easy to assume he's leaving town for good.

By contrast, 'The WASP (Texas Radio and the Big Beat)' is a paean to rock and roll, a studied yet uplifting exultation. Written in 1968 (like 'The Changeling'), this pop voyage of discovery was often incorporated as a route into the group's concerts. According to Krieger, 'It was about the new music Jim heard when his family moved round the South West. He'd got this vision of a huge radio tower spewing out noise . . . this was when XERB was broadcasting and Wolfman Jack was on the air. You could hear him from Tijuana and Tallahassee up to Chicago, where Ray lived. That started rock and roll for our generation.'

Of the other songs on the album, 'Crawling King Snake' is a version of the John Lee Hooker classic, while 'Cars Hiss by my Window' is another punch-drunk evocation of Los Angeles. The LP's centrepiece is 'Riders on the Storm', Morrison's epic swansong. Almost twee in its orchestration, 'Riders on the Storm' is quite sinister, and Morrison's grotesque vocals are deceptively sombre, almost suicidal. Like contemporary records by the Rolling Stones and the Beatles, the Doors' new music was a sad synthesis of exhaustion and regret. This was to be Morrison's last will and testament, truly the end of the road.

'With *LA Woman* he didn't have any more to give,' said Steve Harris, 'he was just wrapping things up. He was completely out of control at this point. We'd go into restaurants and he'd order three meals because he wasn't sure what he wanted. He'd have this big pile of food sitting in front of him and he'd just pick his way through it. Three months before he went to Paris he started to look really rough, rougher than anyone had ever seen him before. He was practically dead at this point. He'd aged ten years, his hair, which was matted and greasy, was starting to recede, and he'd gotten really fat.'

'But although he hated losing his looks,' said Danny Fields, 'in a way he revelled in it, because he was free from the shackles of his own imagined beauty. Towards the end he was far happier with himself, more satisfied with what he had become, and the way he looked. He'd got tired of people expecting to be blown away by this Adonis.'

One song on the album, 'The Changeling', was Morrison's final declaration of independence: here was the fancy-pants chameleon shedding yet another unwanted skin, putting his rock-god days behind him. And this desperation showed like fresh warm sweat on a tight white shirt. This time he was adamant: he was a poet, goddamn it, and people had better believe it. But if, by growing his beard and getting fat, he was moving away from his image as the sexy shaman, the image he was cultivating was not really an image at all. The new Jim Morrison was defined by all the things he no longer wanted to be: he knew what he wasn't, but he wasn't really sure who he *was*.

This confusion led to Morrison's flight to Paris. There he could concentrate on his poetry, hang loose, escape the rush and the push of Los Angeles, and avoid the thousands of temptations awaiting him there. As well as outgrowing the frenetic world of rock and roll, he had finally outgrown his beloved America, no longer looking on the nation as a 'warm neon breast'. He had no reason to stay: he didn't owe Elektra any more product. *Hwy* lacked a distributor, and the continued street hassle of LA was getting to him. In Paris he could be a boulevardier; he could wander the streets, notebook in hand, pop into any of the many cafés and bars and drink himself senseless. And no one would notice.

Now was the time, thought Morrison, to end the Doors once and for all. In an interview with the *Los Angeles Free Press* in November 1970, he told Bob Chorush: 'I think the Doors were very timely. They seem naive now, but a couple of years ago people were into some very weird things. There was a high energy level and we could say things like we did and almost half-ass believe them. We may have been one of the first groups to come along who were openly self-conscious of being performers, and it was reflected in our career as it was happening.'

Steve Harris said, 'It was assumed Jim would go his own way. The band left him alone because they knew he was their meal ticket. He wrote 80 per cent of the material, he was the lead singer, the focal point. It was always Jim. But the others didn't have much of an ego problem, they were too shrewd to want power.'

One of the many things that precipitated the split was Ray Manzarek's obsession with taking the Doors to play in Japan. Manzarek had strong Eastern ties (his wife Dorothy was Japanese) and he wanted the band to immerse itself in its culture. Manzarek told Morrison about the proposed tour, about how it had all been arranged, how it would be great for their creativity and so on. And Morrison, in his deadpan, emotionless way, told Manzarek that not only did he not want anything to do with the proposed Japanese tour, but he also wanted nothing more to do with the group.

Morrison might have had enough of the Doors, but *LA Woman* was greeted with rave reviews by the press, and proved to be their most acclaimed album since *Strange Days*. *Creem* magazine pointed out that 'no other rock group went so dramatically from a position of admiration to sheer hatred in so short a space of time . . . something about them must have rubbed people up the wrong way . . . but *LA Woman* has a more subtle effect, more calm, more resigned . . . than its predecessors.'

During its recording Morrison kept to his usual routine of excessive drinking followed by indiscriminate sex. With Courson away on a tour of Europe, he cruised the bars of downtown LA, getting thrown out of most of them for reciting his poetry, starting fights or molesting girls. He was taking a lot of cocaine, and developed a taste for Scotch. He was still working on a screenplay, but when the words didn't come he consoled himself with booze. He was trying to organise an album through Elektra, and also talked of various movie projects he'd been offered. He'd do anything, he said, to take him away from the Doors.

On 8 December he recorded the poetry which would eventually surface on the posthumous album *An American Prayer*. On 11 and 12 December the Doors played their final concerts, in Dallas and New Orleans. Dallas was quite a success, but his last performance in New Orleans was a shambles, with an almost unrecognisable Morrison stumbling about the stage, mumbling incoherently. He had lost patience with himself and with his audience. According to Manzarek, 'Anyone who was there that night saw it. Jim just . . . lost all his energy halfway into the set. You could almost see it leave him; he hung on to the mike stand and his spirit just slipped away. He was finally drained.'

Alone in LA, Morrison was a danger to himself – he needed Courson or Kennealy to round off the edges. But what he didn't need was both of them together.

This inevitably happened when they both turned up in the city at once, Courson returning from France and Patricia (whom he hadn't seen since before the abortion) flying in from New York. Kennealy, wanting to keep an eye on her man, lodged with Morrison's former publicist Diane Gardiner, who lived directly below Courson's flat in Norton Avenue. Not surprisingly, the two adversaries soon met, and having tried to sort out their differences, ended up talking, drinking and smoking grass together for over three hours.

'I thought Pamela was very sweet,' said Kennealy, 'very pretty, but very young. She had a lot of problems, too. As far as I can tell she never had a proper job in her life . . . I don't know about having an idea in her head. I was disappointed when I met her, I thought perhaps he could have done a bit better. There was this incredible dichotomy – he needed someone like her who he could feel protective towards, but he also had this need to be challenged, and that's what I think he wanted from me. He needed Pamela because she was so vulnerable. It wasn't a relationship of the mind from what I can tell. He needed both of us.'

Morrison came to Courson's apartment that night, only to discover his two regular girlfriends deep in conversation. After all three of them had spent a far-from-uncomplicated evening together, he ended up sleeping with Kennealy, having refused to stay with Courson. For Kennealy this was only a fleeting success, as Morrison spent most of January and February living with Courson.

Kennealy was just too demanding, and Morrison was in no condition to offer anything. To everyone's relief, particularly Morrison's, the band finished recording *LA Woman* during January 1971. Then, on Valentine's Day, Courson flew to Paris to look for an apartment. It was all going according to plan. Kennealy, back in LA after a brief sojourn in Manhattan, stayed with Morrison for a week, seven days of idyllic drunkenness. 'The last week I spent with him,' she said, 'he was charming, a real delight. But the very last time I saw him he was a pig, and the other half took over, so I guess it made it easier in the long run.'

On their final day together, Kennealy and Morrison spent the afternoon in a bar, drinking tequila with beer chasers. Practically paralytic (she remembers having fourteen drinks, and knows she was way behind Morrison) and accompanied by the girl with whom Kennealy was staying, they stumbled over to Poppy Studios, where the rest of the band were mixing the album. Kennealy's room-mate, overawed by being in the presence of such a star, made a successful pass at Morrison, and a while later Patricia discovered them outside on the lawn. A fight broke out.

'It was a stupid fight,' said Kennealy, 'but if I hadn't left I think I would have killed her. It made me so angry that he was making me do this. That was a kind of disengagement, too. I really knew then that I was never going to see him alive again. That was it.'

Morrison's drinking buddy Tom Baker returned from an eight-month sabbatical in London, and with Courson and Kennealy gone, the two of them took to the town, drinking themselves stupid night after night. In the final week before leaving for Paris he slept with a different girl every night. But considering his intake at this point – rumoured to be three bottles of Scotch a day – it is doubtful whether he managed to have sex with any of them.

This was to be the last stage of Morrison's journey into self-inflicted purgatory.

'It consumed him completely at the end,' said Kennealy. 'It was convenient at first, but it overtook him. His persona was ruling his life at the end, and that's why he ran away. That's why he went to Paris.'

For Morrison, Paris was a city of dreamers, of romantics, of poets; his mind raced with thoughts of Rimbaud, Baudelaire, Céline, of Hemingway, Scott Fitzgerald, Picasso and Gertrude Stein; he imagined the Paris of the 1920s, of Montmartre and the Latin Quarter, a Paris of the mind, driven by noble, artistic fervour. It was March, 1971, and this was to be the last stage of Morrison's journey into hell.

Sometimes with Courson, sometimes alone, he'd wander the city, sightseeing, shopping and stopping at dozens of bars. Bar culture in Paris is infinitely better than it is in Los Angeles, and Morrison was in his element. And though he was without his LA buddies, he still managed to attract drinking partners, either fellow expatriates or young, fascinated Parisians. He gained some anonymity, yet his lifestyle hadn't really changed, his scribbled notes being intended now as poems rather than songs. He felt relieved, but also lost and alone, as though he was waving to a crowd that had long since moved on. He walked around Paris in a sweet fog: 'He was drunk a lot . . . that's not to say I never saw him sober, but it usually didn't last,' remembers his biographer Hervé Muller. 'I don't think he was doing anything . . . He had his notebooks and things with him and he was making notes, but I didn't see him working.'

This new life was turning out to be nothing more than an extension of the old one . . . and the binges continued. During this period he only called home twice: once to tell Bill Siddons he'd be staying in Paris longer than the expected six months, and once to John Densmore, just to say hello. To escape from Paris, and his rapidly spreading notoriety, Courson and Morrison hired a car in April and drove down through France to Spain and Morocco, and then in May they flew to Corsica for a ten-day holiday. But back in Paris, the debauchery continued. The end seemed inevitable.

On Friday 2 July, after Morrison had dined with Courson and a friend called Alan Ronay, he took

Courson home, and went alone to the cinema to see *Pursued*, Raoul Walsh's noir Western of 1947, starring Robert Mitchum.

This is where the confusion begins. After the film he is said to have gone to a nightclub, the Rock'n'Roll Circus, and then: (a) overdosed on heroin in the club toilets and been carried back to his apartment, where he passed out in the bathroom; (b) gone back to the apartment, where he complained of being tired and suffered a heart attack in the bath; (c) cruised a few bars before returning home, where he found Courson snorting heroin, joined her, immediately overdosed, the combination of heroin and alcohol proving fatal, and was placed in the bath; or (d) returned home, snorted or injected heroin, then went to lie in a hot bath to savour the full effect. Courson said that he returned home and, after complaining of breathing problems and coughing up a little blood, took a bath. She then went to bed, waking at 5 a.m. to find him still in the bath, dead, with a trickle of blood dripping from one nostril. Due to the intricacies of French law an autopsy was never performed. Though a heart attack was given as the official cause of death, it is now assumed that Morrison almost certainly died from an overdose of heroin. It was to be his final night on the town.

It took a while for the news to reach America, Morrison's death being announced first by the national press in Britain. A UPI statement dated 9 July reads: 'Jim Morrison's death was announced in Los Angeles and confirmed by the American Embassy in Paris. He died last Saturday, 3 July 1971, in Paris. He was staying at 17 Rue Beautreillis with a girlfriend. He complained of feeling sick after a bath and she found him unconscious and called the police physician. He arrived within a few minutes but found Jim dead. The physician announced the death was due to natural causes. He was buried on Wednesday of this week (7 July) at Père Lachaise Cemetery. It is the oldest cemetery in the center of Paris.' Morrison's family having disowned him, Père-Lachaise was Courson's easiest solution.

Immediately, people began to wonder what had really happened. There had been no autopsy, and no one has ever been able to find the doctor who signed the death certificate. No one apart from Courson and the physician saw Morrison placed in the coffin, and Bill Siddons, who flew over to Paris on 6 July after being told of Morrison's death, was confronted with a signed death certificate and a sealed coffin. Because the death was surrounded by controversy, rumours soon began to fly around, mainly about Morrison staging his death and disappearing to North Africa or South America.

It doesn't matter how Jim Morrison died, however, because he really died of self-indulgence. In Paris he had hoped to rise from the ashes of his own humiliation, but he found only self-absorption and, ultimately, death.

The attempt had lasted four months. Jim Morrison's movie was finally over.

Back in the States, Jim Morrison was doing fine with the public – the collection comprising *The Lords* and *The New Creatures* was going into paperback, *LA Woman* was on its way to earning a gold disc, and 'Love Her Madly', taken from it, was the band's biggest hit in two years. But now it was all over, and Morrison had left the theatre. Now it became easier to take him seriously. The twenty-seven-year-old leather man had drunk himself to death, pushed over the finish line by a silly experiment with heroin.

There was nothing else left for him. 'I don't know what would have happened if he'd have come back from Paris,' said Patricia Kennealy. 'He said he was going to come to New York that fall, to concentrate on the films and the poetry, but the Doors say they were convinced he was going back to LA to record another record. He was reaching so desperately at that point for something to hold onto, he could have done anything.'

'It would have been very hard for him to go from being a pop star to a poet,' said Danny Fields. 'He would have been the darling of the poetry world, and he could have been at every poetry reading, published in every little poetry book, because of who he was, but who knows what he could have written? He had such a super-human intelligence, there's no telling what he might have done. That, mixed with maturity and some sense of wisdom, and some freedom from the prison of stardom, might have led to something extremely interesting. But we'll never know.'

Ironically, it was only in death that his biggest wish was realised: his death certificate read: James Douglas Morrison, poet.

As soon as news of Morrison's death hit Los Angeles, various impostors appeared – on the beach, on the radio, at nightclubs, checking into hotels and cashing cheques in his name, even walking into regional newspapers offering exclusives on the disappearance. All this quickly added to the Morrison mystique, the questions about whether or not he was dead, about where he was buried, about how exactly he had died. A web of intricate, interlocking conspiracy theories was rapidly spun, some of which persist to this day.

With Morrison gone, the remaining Doors were unsure about what to do next. At first they were going to call it a day, but soon realised that this would cast Morrison as the only creative element in the group. 'We were insecure,' said Ray Manzarek, 'but we decided to keep on. There was no sense letting it fold up and fall apart. We had too many ideas.'

But, on the strength of their post-Morrison work, this was obviously an untruth.

There was also an air of desperation about the band. Robby Krieger said at the time: 'The reason we're doing it over again is not for the money. It's because what else could we do? It's what we like to do and what we've always done and it's our life. It's just a question of figuring out how to do it.'

So the husk of the band staggered on, releasing two mediocre LPs – *Other Voices* and *Full Circle* – and touring to support them. But without Morrison the music was lifeless. Shocked by his death, Manzarek, Krieger and Densmore turned their back on the dark side of life, and their material became light-hearted and sloppy, as though they were telling themselves that they were human after all. The band shook off their perpetual cloak of fatigue and began smiling in their publicity pictures. 'We've all been down there in the darkness with the heebie-jeebies for the last few years,' said Manzarek, 'and now we finally see the light.' The mood of a Doors concert had previously been intense and austere, but not any more; now the band wore manic, inane grins, as they merrily sauntered through their new material.

It seemed impossible that these were the same men who had been responsible for all that dark, satanic rock – the new music was a strange hybrid of ineffectual jazz-rock and jaunty rock and roll, with no spark. On *Other Voices* and *Full Circle* the band were shown to be the bunch of flyweights they really were, emphasising once again how essential Morrison had been. The public felt the same way, as by themselves, the remaining Doors couldn't get arrested, and their records languished in the lower reaches of the charts. At the end of 1972, inspiration eluding them, and deprived of their single most important element, the band broke up, perhaps finally realising the absurdity of their task.

'We were over in England when we decided to pack in the group,' Manzarek told *Melody Maker* in October 1973. 'Everybody just decided they wanted to pursue their own musical ideas instead of staying together. We went over to England to try and get some new ideas and new blood into the band, be it a new singer, new bass player, new guitarist or whatever, but it didn't happen. It just wasn't right.'

Krieger and Densmore then formed the relatively successful Butts Band, while Manzarek immersed himself in solo work. The Doors once said that trying to replace Morrison would be like trying to replace Jesus: 'It wouldn't have been right. The four of us were so close, the vibrations wouldn't have been right.' But this is what effectively happened when Manzarek drafted Iggy Pop into the ranks.

In 1974 Iggy was in a state of flux; he had moved to Los Angeles after finishing the third and last Stooges album *Raw Power*, and because of his drug problems had split with David Bowie's management company, Mainman. He was alone in LA with no home, no money and no group. Manzarek's manager, Danny

Sugerman, openly wooed Iggy, becoming his manager and convincing him he should work with Manzarek, and eventually the rest of the band. Because of his financial situation, Iggy didn't have a lot of choice, and anyway, Jim Morrison was his hero, the reason he became a singer in the first place. 'Jim Morrison was my idol – if he were alive today, I'd die for him,' he said at the time.

Nothing much came of their collaboration apart from a few impromptu concerts, notably at the LA Palladium and the Whisky a Go Go. At the Whisky gig, on 3 July, the third anniversary of Morrison's death, Iggy went onstage with his hair dyed black, wearing a Jim Morrison T-shirt, and a pair of Morrison's black leather trousers supposedly given to him by Manzarek. He performed a perfunctory set of Doors songs, including 'LA Woman', to which Iggy added these lyrics: 'Jim Morrison died today, Jim Morrison was more beautiful than any girl in this town, and now he's dead, now I cry.'

Iggy once said he was given a trunk full of Morrison's clothes, including many pairs of trousers and the hat Morrison wore at the fatal Miami concert. He showed how much he cared about the Morrison legacy by apparently selling the lot for methadone.

On 25 April 1974 Pamela Courson Morrison died from a heroin overdose, shortly after becoming the legal heir to the Morrison fortune. It probably came as a welcome relief to her: since Morrison's death her days had been overloaded with pain and despair, full of drugs and one-night stands, and she stalked the nightclubs of Los Angeles lost in a twilight world of narcotics and distorted reverie. People were warned not to talk about Morrison in her presence, as she would cry at the very mention of his name. She never seemed to recover from the nightmare of Paris.

'I went to stay with Pamela right after she came back from Paris,' said Danny Fields, 'and she was convinced Jim was living in the dog, she thought his spirit had transferred. The dog would jump up and slobber all over you and she'd say, "Sshhh, Jim's trying to tell you something." I knew then that he was really dead; she wouldn't have been saying that if he was hitchhiking in Arizona. She was in terrible shock, it was so sad.' And when Courson died, the truth about Morrison's death went with her.

The Doors' music would be repackaged and resold throughout the seventies, but it took until 1978 for the legend really to begin to take shape. Since the mid-seventies Manzarek, Krieger and Densmore had been working on the tapes of Morrison's 1970 poetry recitals, providing musical backing for the words; and, along with snippets of original live performances, the results were eventually released as *An American Prayer*. The album was structured as a metaphor for Morrison's life, and, although the verses were more impressive than anything contained in either *The Lords* or *The New Creatures*, it was still less than a vindication of his poetry.

Paul Rothchild told *BAM* magazine's Blair Jackson in 1981, 'That album is a rape ... To me, what was done on *An American Prayer* is the same as taking a Picasso and cutting it into postage-stamp-sized pieces and spreading it across a supermarket wall ... It was the first commercial sell-out of Jim Morrison.'

Patti Smith, talking about the record with Cynthia Rose in January 1979, said, 'His intensity seems dated. Dated in its passion and innocence, like *West Side Story* ... But he was always dated, even when he was around ... He was bigger than life, and so he was laughable. Where does a guy like him fit in?'

In 1979 'The End' finally got its own video: Francis Ford Coppola's Vietnam epic *Apocalypse Now*. Coppola originally asked Manzarek to score an entire soundtrack, but eventually decided instead to feature Morrison's most controversial song over the opening and closing credits (with the vocal substantially remixed by Paul Rothchild). In one scene, not used in the final version, Kurtz, played by Marlon Brando, teaches his private army the words to 'Light My Fire'. The Doors' music was appropriate, not only because it was popular again, but also because it offered an allegorical twist to Coppola's depiction of the war. The movie itself was largely based on Joseph Conrad's *Heart of Darkness*, one of Morrison's favourite books.

As the Jim Morrison legend gained momentum, 1980 saw the release of the exhaustive but sycophantic biography *No One Here Gets Out Alive* – a compelling but ultimately unsatisfying hagiography, written by *Rolling Stone* contributor Jerry Hopkins and the Doors' energetic manager, Danny Sugerman. Hopkins had tried to get his Morrison biography published for years – it was turned down by over thirty publishers but it took Sugerman's overhaul to make it a viable proposition. It was eventually published by Warner Brothers, who had already turned it down twice, and ended up selling millions.

Former Elektra boss Jac Holzman was less than impressed: 'The book was nothing but a repackaging job – not serious. It was too monumental . . . The death rumours? Not sick but unbelievable. Danny Sugerman – how can I phrase this tactfully – wasn't as tight with Jim as you'd think from the book. I doubt if anyone knew Jim *that* well.'

'Hopkins and Sugerman's book is primarily interesting for what it apparently inadvertently reveals,' wrote Lester Bangs. 'In the foreword, on the very first page of the book, Sugerman lets go two sentences which have stopped more than one person of my acquaintance from reading any farther: "I just wanted to say I think Jim Morrison was a modern-day god. Oh hell, at least a lord."

'It was never revealed whether Hopkins shares this assessment, but the authors then go on for almost four hundred pages, amassing mountains of evidence almost all of which can for most readers point to only one conclusion: that Jim Morrison was apparently a nigh-complete asshole from the moment he was born until he died in that bathtub in Paris.

'If Jim Morrison cared so little about his life, was so willing to make it amount to one huge alcoholic exhibitionistic joke, why should they or we or anybody finally care, except insofar as the seamy details provide trashy entertainment?'

By the following year, the tenth anniversary of Morrison's death, the revival was in full swing. In July Manzarek, Krieger and Densmore led fans in a grave-side tribute ceremony at Père-Lachaise; in September the compilation LP *The Doors' Greatest Hits* went platinum in the USA; and *Rolling Stone* was one of seven magazines to put the dead Door on their front cover. ('He's Hot, He's Sexy, And He's Dead', screamed the cover line.) This was the fourth time Morrison had made the cover of *Rolling Stone*, the second time post-humously. In 1981 more Doors records were sold than in any year since they were first released. Teenagers discovered the band for the first time, their records went into heavy rotation on college-radio stations all over America, and they soon became as popular as the Rolling Stones or Van Halen. Big Jim had risen again, creeping into every suburban bedroom with his dirty lyrics and unsettling white-man's blues. The youth of America again asked Morrison to carry the black flag for them, and he was powerless to resist. Morrison's death took on a life of its own, and the Doors, with Danny Sugerman marketing the myth, experienced an extraordinary renaissance.

In the years since then there have been more records, more books, more videos, Oliver Stone's movie, more discoveries of lost poetry, and more posthumous deifi-cation. Now, over forty years after his death, Morrison fever is everywhere. Documentaries are being edited, records being compiled, T-shirts and posters still being printed in their millions. The Morrison industry is thriving. Jim Morrison's image is stronger than ever, and, no matter what comes to light, nothing seems able to tarnish that image. Wherever you go in the world, there will always be a screenprinted image of the tortured icon staring out at you from the front of a T-shirt, trapped for ever in a freeze-framed grimace.

Morrison was the sexiest bookworm to ever pick up a microphone, he was an inspired lyricist and one of the most celebrated pop icons of the sixties. But he was also a wilfully enigmatic, pretentious loud-mouth, a self-proclaimed poet who wore the mask of the drunk. He was the impotent alcoholic, the scarred idol. He was the King of Corn, the consummate showman, the petulant clown. He was too clever for his own good, and often too stupid to care. Masochist, emotional sadist, incurable romantic – Morrison was all these things. But the T-shirts don't have room for any of them, instead promoting only the image of the gaunt, all-conquering sex beast, the Crawling King Snake, the Killer on the Road, the Lord of the Dance, the Lizard King, Mr Mojo Risin'.

'Towards the end he had complete contempt for his audience,' said Patricia Kennealy, 'because they couldn't see what he wanted to do. He had this idea that he could lead them after him like a pig on a stick, but they weren't really following. He became disillusioned when they only picked up on the sensationalist stuff, the stuff he used to gain their attention. They didn't understand him, and it was partly his fault.'

As a role model for pop stars, Morrison has been enormously influential, and in the last forty years his legend has been interpreted by hundreds of performers, both good and bad. His whole persona – his passion, his intellect, his pretensions and his cynicism – quickly became a rock and roll blueprint, one that's been relentlessly copied. As Steve Harris said, 'He really did invent a way of looking back at the world.' He not only inspired a generation of delinquents, he also provided them with a game plan. If, during his life, he had become a mirror for his audience, after his death he became a mirror for his mimics. Many have been inspired by Morrison's poetic visions and tormented make-up, while others have abused his ironic stage mannerisms – particularly Alice Cooper, who exploited Morrison's uneasy, cathartic performances and cold-heartedly formularised them, turning himself into a moneymaking freak show in the process.

David Bowie, Iggy Pop, Patti Smith, Julian Cope, Echo and the Bunnymen's Ian McCulloch and Joy Division's Ian Curtis are among the most pertinent imitators, though Curtis is one of the few to have taken his role to its tragic conclusion, killing himself in 1980. His death also created its own absurd mythology, his fans interpreting personal torment as artistic frustration and futility.

But for many rock stars, the problem of what to do when they turn thirty remains a huge problem. If you start out angry and alienated, what's the point of growing old gracefully? What kind of a legacy is that? Shouldn't you just kill yourself through overindulgence?

'In a way, Jim Morrison's life and death could be written off as simply one of the more pathetic episodes in the history of the star system,' said Lester Bangs, 'or that offensive myth we all persist in believing which holds that artists are somehow a race apart and thus entitled to piss on my wife, throw you out the window, smash up the joint and generally do whatever they want. I've seen a lot of this over the years, and what's most ironic is that it always goes under the assumption that to deny them these outbursts would somehow be curbing their creativity, when the reality, as far as I can see, is that it's exactly such insane tolerance of another insanity that also contributes to their drying up as artists. Because how can you finally create anything real or beautiful when you have absolutely zero input from the real world, because everyone around you is catering to and sheltering you?'

Morrison is now considered to be one of the few genuine rock and roll archetypes, whose behaviour has been copied remorselessly by at least two generations of equally obnoxious but uniformly less talented frontmen – mere chimps to Morrison's eight-hundred-pound gorilla. Using Jim Morrison as a role model is ultimately unsuccessful because those who do are ever reliant on their six-gear anti-social tendencies disguising their creative shortcomings (actions trumping language). Whereas Morrison's absurdity blossomed into majesty, attempts to mimic him are always belittled by cliché.

Jim Morrison got out before he was found out. Because he disappeared when he was only twenty-seven, he left no clues as to how today's dark stars should spend their thirties, let alone the rest of their lives. What would he have done? Would he have deteriorated like Elvis Presley, or found God like Bob Dylan? Or would he have become a parody of himself – something he was already in danger of doing – like John Lydon, Mick Jagger or Pete Townshend?

Perhaps he would have faded into obscurity, like so many other stars of the sixties. It is impossible to say whether poetry – Morrison's first love and second career – would have granted him the dignity he desired, the dignity he had lost through the Doors' success.

Possibly he would have been disgusted by his own shortcomings. Steve Harris, at least, was convinced about what would have happened: 'He would have split the group, and become a down-and-out alcoholic. He would have tried to sober up, he would have lost his hair and gotten a paunch. It would have been downhill all the way. He would have tried directing movies, but they would have been marginal. He would never have been able to star in a movie, his looks just wouldn't have allowed it.'

But, had he lived, and had he been able to come to terms with his previous success, it's possible that Morrison would have been a much happier, far more complete person; for his fans, though, this would have been a disaster, as he would have grown up in public. Rock and roll obsessives don't want career plans, they want starbursts and crash landings . . . and with Jim Morrison they got exactly that. For them, the singer will always be twenty-something; he'll never denounce the booze, or give up the good life. Morrison will never change, and that's just the way they like it.

Ultimately Jim Morrison's blueprint is incomplete, being no more than the distillation of an impassioned, violent, misspent youth.

Which is why he remains a hero, a pop deity: time didn't allow Morrison to grow old in public, and so his life remains a prototype of immaturity. We worship Jimi Hendrix, Sid Vicious, Jim Morrison, Ian Curtis and Kurt Cobain because they didn't allow time to interfere with their ambitions; in death they are, to quote Morrison himself, 'stoned, immaculate'. In rock and roll, it seems, the dead will always have the edge on the living.

7

Père-Lachaise Redux

And alien tears will fall for him,
Pity's long broken urn,
For his mourners will be outcast men
And outcasts always mourn

Inscription on Oscar Wilde's tomb at Père-Lachaise

On a bright and sunny but deceptively cold winter afternoon, a crowd of mourners are standing beside Jim Morrison's grave. They are here because today is a special day – Morrison's birthday. Six miniature champagne bottles sit atop his tombstone, as do a few handwritten letters and about a dozen bouquets of flowers. On the surrounding graves there is some new graffiti, though nothing radically different from what's already scrawled there: 'Yo, Lizard King', 'Free dope for ever', 'You are stoned, do you feel your limbs? You are dead', 'Nico loved you, but she died', 'Girls! Girls! Girls!', 'Wine, best you want', 'The door in the West is closed', 'Sex and drugs and Doors', 'It's better to burn out than fade away', 'Hotel Morrison, occupied', 'Burn both ends!'.

A Frenchwoman in her late thirties stares intently at these pledges to hedonism, and then drops a single red rose onto the grave before running off. She shakes her head as I approach her. For her, at least, this is a private visit.

It might be Morrison's birthday, but today is pretty much the same as any other at Père-Lachaise. There are no TV crews, no huge groups of worshippers – only the odd tourist, a few tokens of remembrance and the inevitable litter. Hugh, a student from Bristol, is disappointed. 'I thought there'd be more people here,' he says. 'I'm a big fan of Jim's, and I thought his other fans would be here too.' He arrived from Britain this morning, and will be leaving later this afternoon. It's his first time in Paris, and he won't be visiting anywhere else – 'What's the point? This is what I came for.'

Janette Cutter is from Connecticut, and her two-month tour of Europe is just beginning. 'I'm here with a bunch of college friends. When we decided to come, Jim Morrison's grave was the one thing which we all had to see. It was our only definite plan.'

Today is also her birthday – her twenty-first – and she's giving Morrison the bunch of red roses given to her this morning. 'I think he's so cool, you know? I like his poetry, I have his poem books, and I thought it would be a neat thing to come today, because it's our birthday. I'd read about the grave before, but it's kinda disgusting. I met someone last night whose father's buried near here, and he hates the graffiti on his grave. It says 'Jim this way', and he's kinda offended by that.'

The tourists come and go, carrying the ubiquitous accessories for sightseeing in Paris: cameras and bottles of Evian. A look of disappointment tends to cross their faces when they appear at the grave. Paris's fourth most popular tourist attraction is certainly an underwhelming sight. Being a Saturday, tomorrow will be busier, and Jackie will be here. Forty-year-old Jackie comes every Saturday, at 11 a.m., to clean and to tidy the grave. She brings a bottle of champagne or Jim Beam, and sits on a nearby stone, talking to herself in her quiet Parisienne voice, ignoring those around her.

Jackie, and others like her, is one of the people Michelle Campbell sees here regularly. Michelle, an American in her mid-thirties, has been photographing Père-Lachaise cemetery every day since January, a personal project which she hopes to have published. 'I was here for the anniversary of his death in July, and it was crazy. There were about fifty of these really drunk German fans, singing at the top of their voices. That's when the obsessives come out of the woodwork.

'Earlier in the year they had five guards around the grave all day, though they let up in the summer. Sometimes they try and hide the grave, or tell people he's not buried here anymore. They hate the mess, and the graffiti. They really wish he was gone.'

At four o'clock the day draws to a close. The wind pushes the leaves through the pathways and the avenues in between the graves, like a cheap effect in a pop video. It's time to go. There is nothing more to see. Tomorrow, the next day, and the day after that, more people will arrive. Some will pass by in minutes, while others will moon about the dead dark star, dressed from head to toe in black, paying homage to the original rock and roll wastrel, hoping some of Morrison's stardust falls their way.

As Michelle turns to go, she beckons me over: 'I was here in August, and this American guy turns up with his two young daughters. One of them asks him why a Traveling Wilbury is buried in France. On being told that Morrison wasn't in the band, she says, "You mean this isn't Roy Orbison?" I think it was the only dead rock star she knew. Another time, there were these American college students here, and this one girl says, at the top of her voice, "Wow, what a concept of death. He coulda had any stone he wanted, he was rich, man, and look at what he chose. What a concept."'

Bibliography

Balfour, Victoria, *Rock Wives*, Beech Tree Books, 1986

Bangs, Lester, *Psychotic Reactions and Carburetor Dung*, Heinemann, 1988

Christgau, Robert, *Any Old Way You Choose It*, Penguin, 1973

Cohn, Nik, *Awopbopaloobop Alopbamboom*, Weidenfeld & Nicolson, 1969

Crosby, David and Carl Gottlieb, *Long Time Gone*, Heinemann, 1989

Des Barres, Pamela, *I'm With the Band*, Pamela Des Barres, Beech Tree Books, 1987

Doe, Andrew and John Tobler, *The Doors in Their Own Words*, Omnibus Press, 1988

Farren, Mick, *The Black Leather Jacket*, Plexus, 1985

Green, Jonathan, *Days in the Life*, Minerva, 1988

Harman, Gary, *Rock'n'Roll Babylon*, Plexus, 1982

Hopkins, Jerry and Danny Sugerman, *No One Here Gets Out Alive*, Warner Books, 1980

Jahn, Mike, *Jim Morrison and the Doors*, Grosset & Dunlap, 1969

Jones, Mablen, *Getting It On: The Clothing of Rock'n'Roll*, Abbeville Press, 1987

Lisciandro, Frank, *Jim Morrison, An Hour for Magic*, Delilah, 1982

Morrison, Jim, *The Lords and The New Creatures*, Omnibus, 1985

Morrison, Jim, *Lyrics and Poems*, Stampa Alternativa, 1989

Morrison, Jim, *Wilderness: The Lost Writings of Jim Morrison*, Villard, 1988

Nilsen, Per and Dorothy Sherman, *Iggy Pop: The Wild One*, Omnibus, 1988

Peellaert, Guy and Nik Cohn, *Rock Dreams*, Popular Library, 1973

Stallings, Penny, *Rock'n'Roll Confidential*, Vermilion, 1984

Stein, Jean, *Edie*, Jonathan Cape, 1982

Sugerman, Danny, *The Doors: The Illustrated History*, Omnibus Press, 1983

Sugerman, Danny, *Wonderland Avenue*, Sidgwick & Jackson, 1989

Tobler, John and Andrew Doe, *The Doors*, Bobcat Books, 1984

Various, *The Day the Music Died*, Plexus, 1989

Warhol, Andy and Pat Hackett, *POPism: The Warhol Sixties*, Harcourt, Brace, Jovanovich, 1980

Williams, Paul, *Outlaw Blues*, E.P. Dutton & Co., 1969

Magazine articles
Bell, Max, 'Weird Scenes Inside the Goldmine', *NME*, 1975

Breslin, Rosemary, Jerry Hopkins and Paul Williams, 'He's Hot, He's Sexy, He's Dead', *Rolling Stone*, 1981

Dorrell, David, 'Mr Mojo Rises Again', *NME*, 1983

Farren, Mick, 'The Hunting of the Lizard King', *NME*, 1975

Zwerin, Michael, 'The Jim Morrison Bust', *Cheetah*, 1968

BIBLIOGRAPHY

'The 100 Best Singles of the Last 25 Years', *Rolling Stone*, 1988

Articles from: *RAM, Cheetah, Crawdaddy, Creem, Dark Star, Doors Quarterly, Eye, Guardian, Keyboards and Music Player, Los Angeles Free Press, Melody Maker, Newsweek, New York, New York Times, Passion, Record Mirror, Sounds, Time, Village Voice, American Vogue, Way Ahead*

Films

Dance On Fire, CIC, 1985

The Doors Are Open, Granada, 1968

The Doors in Europe, Castle Hendring, 1989

Live at the Hollywood Bowl, Doors Video Co., 1987

A Tribute to Jim Morrison, Warner Brothers, 1981

Radio series

The Doors from the Inside, produced by Sandy Gibson

Acknowledgements

With thanks to Ed Victor, Nigel Newton, Jonathan Newhouse, Karl Badger, Max Bell, Maurice Boland, Gordon Burn, Robert Christgau, Nik Cohn, Nicholas Coleridge, John Densmore, Robin Derrick, Pamela Des Barres, Jeff Dexter, Tony Elliott, Danny Fields, Kathryn Flett, Steve Harris, Jerry Hopkins, Alice Howarth, Nick Humphrey, Terry and Tricia Jones, David Keeps, Patricia Kennealy-Morrison, Nick Kent, Robby Krieger, Nick Logan, Christian Logan Wright, Ray Manzarek, Jim McClellan, Haoui Montaug, Lisa Nesselson, Lee Ellen Newman, The New York Public Library, Tony Parsons, Tony Peake, John Peel, David Reynolds, Helen Ridge, Alix Sharkey, Stephanie Sleap, Neil Spencer, Danny Sugerman, James Truman, John Williams, and to Sarah, Edie, Georgia, Audrey and Mike.

Index

INDEX